INTRODUCTION TO PERT

R. STANSBURY STOCKTON

CONSULTING EDITOR

THE ALLYN AND BACON
SERIES IN QUANTITATIVE
METHODS FOR BUSINESS
AND ECONOMICS

ALLYN AND BACON, INC.

BOSTON   1964

M

INTRODUCTION TO

PERT

HARRY F. EVARTS

Assistant Dean

College of Business Administration

Ohio University

Z29908

PREFACE

INTRODUCTION TO PERT was written for students of business administration. A version of this material was first presented in both undergraduate and graduate production management courses at Northwestern University, to introduce students to PERT, one of the most widely used new quasi-mathematical management techniques. A basic objective of these courses was to train students to understand the commonly used management techniques, their natures, uses, strengths, and weaknesses.

Like other new management science techniques, of which linear programming is a prime example, PERT has wide application; it is not limited to production, although it was introduced and is still very useful there. PERT is used in marketing, maintenance, research and development, merger or acquisition, securities issues, advertising, and the like.

An oft-cited reason for omitting the new quantitative techniques from business curriculums is that students do not have the needed mathematical background for dealing with them. PERT does not suffer from this limiting factor; in fact, except for a touch of sophistication which requires a nodding acquaintance with statistics, no mathematics is required. If elected, PERT can be both taught and appreciated without one's having to go into the technical statistical analysis such as that presented in the last section of Chapter 3 of this book. This operational and conceptual simplicity, when combined with its ability to generate multiple and varied data, accounts for the explosive growth in the use of PERT.

Heretofore, no textbooks on PERT have been published. There have, however, been many articles (including a collection published by the American Management Association), several United States Government monographs (notably from the Bureau of Naval Weapons), and a number of reports from technical departments of companies which use PERT. These publications tend to fall into two categories: completely detailed technical descriptions, heavily weighted with complex mathematical notation (despite the dearth of mathematics in the technique itself); and very simplified versions, usually prepared to give busy executives a quick insight into the nature of PERT. The former are excellent study materials for PERT practitioners or persons who plan to become such, but they are clearly too demanding for business school students with respect to time required for attainment of the necessary skill level. The simplified versions, although rather easily understood, provide no problems or practice and thus tend to gloss over the operational difficulties of using PERT.

Introduction to PERT is an intermediate presentation. It omits all except the essential symbolic notation and uses in its place common business terminology. A number of questions and problems are provided to reinforce learning. As the title implies, the book is an introduction to PERT, not an exhaustive treatment. A selected bibliography is provided for those who wish to pursue the subject in greater depth.

This book could not have been written without the contributions of many organizations and individuals. Jack Stolle and Jack Warren of Booz·Allen & Hamilton provided very generously of their time and vast experience with PERT. Bill Park uncomplainingly allowed me to follow his actions for what must have appeared to be endless weeks. Al Morris of the Northwestern University Computing Center put the computer programs "on the air." Kenneth H. Myers of Northwestern University was the book's first booster and a most interested supporter. Douglass Mann opened the Kitchens of Sara Lee Company, graciously supplied valuable and helpful information for this study, and has supported the project from the beginning. To all of these men I owe many thanks.

No book is produced without an editor, and my wife Dru provided her expert generalship for this one. Dorothy Scanlan cheerfully learned a dozen new skills (such as key punch operation, drafting, PERT calculations) while surviving the several manuscript drafts.

Gratitude is also due the hundreds of Northwestern University students who were experimented upon with drafts of the material in this book. And, as is their custom when aid is requested by universities, 22 American companies, including the IBM Corporation, contributed brochures, manuals, and computer programs to this effort.

Harry F. Evarts

CONTENTS

ix

3

COMPUTATIONAL PROCEDURE   45

1 ▸ INTRODUCTION

1.1 BACKGROUND

NEW MANAGEMENT TECHNIQUES have been developed and accepted rapidly in recent years. PERT (Program Evaluation and Review Technique), introduced in 1958, is one of the most widely used.

PERT was created in an effort to achieve a drastic reduction in the time span originally projected for the development of the Polaris Ballistic Missile, the primary weapon of the United States Navy's fleet of atomic submarines and a major factor in our nation's defense program. PERT was developed and applied in a joint project by representatives of the Navy Special Projects Office, Lockheed Aircraft Corporation, and Booz·Allen & Hamilton, a prominent management consulting firm in Chicago. PERT is credited with being instrumental in cutting years from the Polaris development program. The success of the Polaris missile itself is well known.

1

1.2 DEFINITION

PERT is a planning and control technique with quantitative embellishments. Its fundamental analytical device is the network, a pictorial representation of the work necessary to reach an objective. The network and the use of statistics and computers distinguish PERT from other planning and control techniques.

PERT is designed to evaluate progress toward the attainment of project goals, focus attention on potential and actual problems in projects, provide management with frequent, accurate status reports, predict likelihood of reaching project objectives, and determine the shortest time in which a project can be completed.

The simple network in Figure 1.1 shows "how PERT looks." Full explanations of the various parts of a network and how they are made up will be found in succeeding chapters.

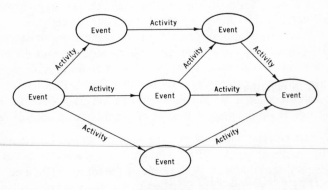

Figure 1.1

1.3 NEED

While Adam Smith's pin factory[1] is not the first recorded instance of management's planning the work of employees, it is among

---

[1] Adam Smith, *The Wealth of Nations*. New York: Random House, 1937, pp. 3–12.

the most often cited. The introduction of such management planning activities resulted in greatly increased productivity. But it had a byproduct as well, greatly increased complexity in business management. Someone had to do the necessary planning, supervising, and controlling.

Management's answer to the problem was to create a staff with the responsibility and authority to carry out the planning of work force activities. With the passage of time, more and more specialized staff organizations were added, significantly so in the early part of this century when scientific management became popular.

The most recent and consistent contributor to the complexity of business management has been technological change, which now occurs much more rapidly than it has in the past. Previously, time gaps existed between the stages of innovation, and a manager could expect respite between the phases of research, design, engineering, assembly of resources, production, and distribution. Today's faster-developing and more competitive business world allows no such luxury. These phases usually overlap; in fact, the time spans of several parts of the various phases may run concurrently.

It comes as no surprise, then, to learn that management quickly utilizes every new technique that promises to ease the problems associated with innovation, rapidity of technological change, and planning and controlling business operations. PERT is one of these techniques and, as experience has shown, is a powerful new weapon in the management arsenal of planning and control techniques.

1.4   THE MANAGER AND PERT

Because PERT has so many industrial applications, knowledge of its operation and application is highly advisable for managers today. While the use of this technique has grown rapidly, line managers' lack of understanding of it appears to be the major factor limiting even more rapid growth.

Successful use of PERT by line managers requires an "administrative point of view." They do not need skill in the actual practice of the technique, this being the forte of the PERT analyst.

What they do need is ability to recognize uses for it. Moreover, they need to be able to mobilize resources, to evaluate and interpret results, and most important, to make decisions and take action as a consequence of the data generated through the use of PERT.

1.5   USES

Although PERT can be applied to many management tasks to achieve lower costs and reduce project time and manpower needs, its values are most apparent in project-type activities which tend to be conducted only once or twice, and which are not routine or repetitive operations. PERT also shows itself to advantage in complex programs which have many tasks, interdependencies, and interrelationships to be considered. In addition, PERT is the best approach to new, untried activities not easily likened to past experiences.

PERT has been put to many nondefense uses such as industrial research and development and heavy or "engineered" construction of bridges, buildings, power stations, and dams. Uses of PERT which are still gaining in popularity include computer programming and installation; preparation of bids and proposals; shutting down and restarting of chemical plants, blast furnaces, oil refineries, and similar installations where periodic maintenance shutdowns are required; installation of production control systems; start-up of standby production facilities; pilot production runs; and production facility changeover for new models. Some uses are shown in Figure 1.2.

While it is true that PERT's first uses were military and its first industrial uses were in the area of production, the tool is now much more widely employed. Most of the new management science techniques have followed similar patterns of growth and usage. Some potential applications for PERT are advertising programs, securities issues, introduction of new products, mergers or acquisitions, and marketing plans.

It should be remembered that PERT deals only with the time constraint and does not include the quantity, quality, and cost information desired in many projects; PERT should, therefore, be

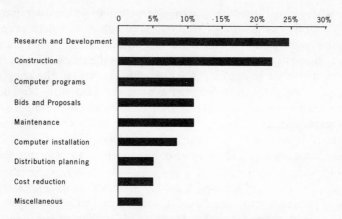

Figure 1.2 Distribution of PERT uses. (SOURCE: Booz · Allen & Hamilton, Inc., Management Research Department)

integrated with other methods of planning and control. It can replace only a few of them. Considerable effort is being expended to integrate the techniques of PERT with such other methods as line of balance, resource allocation, and manpower scheduling, as well as to incorporate cost analysis. More on this subject can be found in Chapter 5.

1.6 ADVANTAGES OF PERT

Many characteristics of PERT have made it an increasingly popular instrument of management. Six are outstanding:

1. Creation of a realistic, detailed, easy-to-communicate plan which greatly improves the chances for attainment of project objectives.

2. Prediction of time and uncertainties of performance.

3. Attention focused on parts of a project which are most likely to impede or delay its achievement.

4. Information provided about project resources that are not being fully utilized.

5. Simulation of alternative plans and schedules.

6. Provision of thorough and frequent project status reports.

PERT methodology demands and forces complete project planning and from this follows the first advantage mentioned above, the creation of a realistic plan which improves the chances for attainment of project objectives. Anyone who has written the simplest computer program, or calculated a work standard with Methods-Time-Measurement, or taken a trial balance will be reminded of that experience as he works with PERT because PERT has the same types of interrelationships which demand complete consideration. The consequence of failure to plan completely is an incorrect solution.

The ability of the PERT user to predict time and uncertainties of performance in the future makes it a remarkable addition to the kit of management tools. Many PERT enthusiasts employ the technique only because it can be used to determine the shortest time in which a project can be completed. Prior to the introduction of PERT, estimates of project duration were notoriously inaccurate. Even though statistical embellishments make PERT somewhat complicated, it enables the user to predict a completion date with a measure of certainty, and to make this prediction even before the project begins. In addition, estimates can be revised constantly while work is in progress.

Focusing attention on the parts of the project that are most likely to prevent its success is another important characteristic of PERT. This is an extension of the principle of managing by exception, which in the past has not been possible in tasks of the type for which PERT is most useful.

PERT also provides information about project resources that are not being fully utilized. In many of these instances, the underused resources can be applied to parts of the project which may otherwise hold up total completion.

With relatively little effort, many alternative methods of planning and scheduling a project can be simulated. The speed and accuracy of simulation with PERT are far superior to those of any previous method used and simulation can be accomplished at very small cost. Since the cost is negligible, simulation can be carried out for even the most questionable alternatives and it can be done at any time during the life of the project.

As for the final advantage, that of frequent status reports, PERT can hardly be outdone. Daily reports are entirely possible if they are desired. In contrast to the possibilities available with other project control techniques, which provide only historical information, the PERT user can describe current status and predict future performance as well as point out potential trouble spots. This characteristic, coupled with the user's ability to establish and maintain interrelationships of project components, makes the feature of frequent status reports one of PERT's most outstanding.

1.7   COSTS AND SAVINGS

There is something of the pack instinct among businessmen. When a few leaders adopt something new which appears to have promise, many others follow without a thorough appraisal of the issues. Such was the case in the headlong race to adopt computers in the 1950s. Few computer installations could have been justified on a hard-headed preliminary economic analysis, yet very few have been proved to be poor economic investments. (Whoever heard of a computer's being removed—except to be replaced by a larger computer?)

In some respects PERT's widespread use is a consequence of the pack instinct. In some companies it has been adopted without a comprehensive analysis. Yet there are few dissatisfied PERT users, and those that do find fault with the technique appear to have misunderstood its possibilities to the extent of expecting too much.

Clearly, one of the important reasons for acceptance has been its low cost relative to the savings achieved. The direct costs of PERT are:

1. salary of the analyst(s);
2. consulting service (if any); and
3. computer time.

The largest indirect cost is the value of the alternative use of the effort of the many persons who contribute time, facts, and judgments necessary for the use of PERT. Depending upon the magnitude of the project, this may include some of the time of 50 percent of the management. The time spent can involve contributing time estimates, checking the sequence logic of events, or any number of other involvements up to monitoring project progress through checking PERT output reports. For all practical purposes, the indirect costs cannot be calculated.

Navy officials state that PERT adds only about one-tenth of 1 percent to a contract price.[2] The Air Force indicates that the cost is about one-half of 1 percent of the total cost of a research and development project.[3] In the author's experience, nonmilitary users of PERT usually place the cost at a nominal "less than 1 percent of project cost." It should be remembered that the costs of PERT usually are not added costs because in most applications PERT replaces another less systematic planning and control device.

The savings made possible by PERT are even more difficult to ascertain than are the costs. Who could calculate the value of having nine Polaris missile submarines on station by the end of 1962 instead of one by the end of 1963? The latter was the Navy's objective before the advent of PERT. What is the value to a computer manufacturer when he is able to achieve a 50 percent time reduction on the development of a medium-size computer, and thus is able to top the market by two months?

Literature in the field lacks specific comments about the savings realized through PERT.[4] At this stage the reader must be satisfied that the savings far outshadow the costs.

1.8 THE PERT ANALYST

The first step by any manager who wants to use PERT is the development of an analyst. Such a person will probably have to be "home-grown"; few are available in the employment market. There are, however, a number of consulting firms that now have PERT

---

[2] Howard Simons, "PERT: How to Meet a Deadline," *Think*, Vol. 28, No. 5, pp. 13–17. May, 1962.
[3] *The Management Implications of PERT* (Chicago: Booz·Allen & Hamilton, Inc., 1962), p. 19.
[4] A single exception exists: "In private industry for the management of a new product activity . . . savings on the order of 20% have been claimed." D. G. Malcolm, "PERT—A Designed Management Information System," *Proceedings of the Industrial Management Society Special Conference*, Chicago: Industrial Management Society, October 11–12, 1960, pp. 1–12.

capability and an increasing number of professional associations (American Management Association, American Institute of Industrial Engineers) who present PERT training programs. The curriculums of many university business administration programs now include instruction in PERT.

Certain characteristics make one person more desirable than another as a PERT analyst. Three seem outstanding:

1.   Broad industrial experience. The ability to understand the language of the many persons who provide data for the project is a vital part of this characteristic. When an industrial engineer tells him that a reject rate at heat treat of greater than 4.5 percent will unbalance the assembly line, the PERT analyst must be able to grasp the implications of this information as they affect the total project.

2.   Ability to work with both higher- and lower-placed personnel in other departments. The necessary data are contributed by many persons and PERT reports are used at several levels of management. Therefore the analyst should have a personality that can inspire the confidence of and develop rapport with persons of differing personalities occupying assorted organizational posts.

3.   An analytical and receptive mind. Change is the only constant in American industry today and PERT is its constant witness. Old practices and procedures are falling by the wayside and new ones are under continuous revision. The analyst should be capable of seeing needs and opportunities in this light and should be willing to do so.

1.9   PLAN OF STUDY

Presentation of material in this book is designed for an orderly build-up into a usable understanding of PERT. Technical aspects are discussed in Chapters 2 and 3. These include network design, the critical path concept, and calculations. Network analysis and administrative aspects, such as organizational relationships and some human problems caused by innovation, make up Chapter 4. The future and the relationships of PERT to development of planning and control techniques in general are the subjects of Chapter 5.

The time needed to train a PERT analyst is variously esti-
mated at three to six months. Clearly, a thorough reading of this
book could not create such an expert. But the reader will be able
to appreciate the applications of PERT, to design and calculate
simple networks, and to understand how PERT is used as a planning
and control device.

1.10   QUESTIONS

1. Is PERT expensive to use? Explain.

2. The text describes three desirable characteristics of a PERT analyst.
    What other characteristics would you consider desirable?

3. How is PERT different from other planning and control techniques
    with which you are familiar?

4. Cite examples from marketing, production, and finance in which
    PERT would be a useful management technique.

2 ▸ THE PERT NETWORK

2.1 INTRODUCTION

IF A BOARD CHAIRMAN calls a meeting, he prepares an agenda. If a foreman is going to produce a part, he determines which machines will be employed in its manufacture. If a college professor begins a book, he makes an outline.

Similarly, if a businessman is about to embark on a new business operation, he should assemble all the information pertinent to the project and then order and use the information logically.

The initial activities of all these persons can be summed up in one word: planning. The discussion in this chapter centers around the PERT network, a project planning device.

2.2 PROJECT OBJECTIVE

The first step in developing a PERT network is to specify clearly the project objective. At first this may appear a superfluous statement, but meeting this requirement takes a great deal of thought. It is not adequate to say that the objective is to tear down and rebuild a papermaking machine; or to create, test, and sell a new cereal; or to build a new factory. The objective must be stated as specifically as possible and should include adequate specifications in writing so that all persons who have responsibilities in the project will be fully informed.

Thus if the project is a new factory building, the minimal specifications to be stated along with the objective would include location, completion date, site plan, building plans, building materials, heat-light-power specifications, and grading and landscaping plans. Making and executing the necessary arrangements for these specifications would naturally lead to completion of the building—the final objective which would become the end event in the PERT network.

2.3 BAR CHARTS

A PERT network has been defined as a pictorial representation of a project. Before the advent of PERT, there were other attempts to display graphically the activities that comprised projects. The most widely used was the bar chart, also referred to as the Gantt

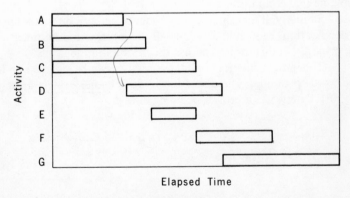

Elapsed Time

Figure 2.1

chart.[1] Bar charts depict the occurrence of activities in parallel or in series over a time period, as in Figure 2.1.

Activities represented by overlapping bars can be accomplished concurrently, at least to the extent of the overlap. Activities represented by bars in series (i.e., an earlier bar stops before the later one begins) usually must be accomplished in the sequence indicated. For instance, Activity D in Figure 2.1 cannot begin until Activity A is completed.

In practice, bar charts have serious limitations. Consider Figure 2.2, a bar chart depicting construction of a house. Everything appears to be going well. All activities except millwork are on or ahead of schedule. The delay in millwork seems no cause for alarm, since the project still has three weeks to run, and the chart shows only two weeks of millwork left to complete.

But the vital fact that cannot be made clear in this type of chart is the interdependency of the various activities. The mere fact that they are scheduled for simultaneous or overlapping times does not make them necessarily related or interdependent.

At this point of time in question here, the interior decorator has completed his first week of work on schedule despite the fact that

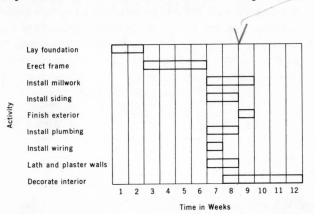

Figure 2.2 (SOURCE: K. L. Deane, "Fundamentals of Network Planning and Analysis," Remington Rand Univac Division, January, 1962)

---

[1] After Henry Gantt, a scientific management pioneer, who introduced bar charts around the turn of the century.

the millwork contractor is behind. Now the question arises whether the interior decorator can proceed, or if more work on his part is dependent on the millwork contractor's being on schedule. If the latter is the case, the completion date of the entire project will extend beyond the schedule because of the fact that the millwork is now behind. The chart shows that the interior decorator will have two *3* weeks' work after the millwork contractor is finished. If the two are interrelated, the final completion date will run over by one week. However, if they are independent, at least to the extent that the interior decorater could work around the millwork contractor, this overage in completion time might not arise or might not amount to the total time lost by the millwork contractor.

Clearly, because of these limitations, bar charts are only partially useful planning and control devices.

2.4 BAR CHARTS TO NETWORKS

The steps from bar charts to networks of the type used with PERT actually made up a form of evolution. One of the developments in the evolutionary process was the milestone chart. On the bar chart (Figure 2.2), it is indicated that the foundation must be laid before the frame can be constructed. The frame must be completed before the millwork, siding, plumbing, wiring, or plastering can begin. The reader of the chart could get the impression that all five of these activities could be carried on at once. This is only partially true. For example, some millwork would cover up some plaster; therefore completion of some of the millwork is dependent upon completion of some of the plastering. This dependency cannot be shown on the bar chart. It is true that the millwork bar extends one week beyond the lathing and plastering bar, but the observer cannot be sure just *what* plastering or *what* millwork will be accomplished *when*.

This difficulty points up another deficiency of the bar chart as a planning device. The bars are of such length that it is difficult to define precisely the work being accomplished at any specific time. For example, "decorate interior" covers four weeks. There may be six or eight rooms to be decorated, but the bar does not show the specific order of progression.

The bar chart also has limitations as a control device. Figure 2.3 is the same bar chart as is Figure 2.2, except that it has become a project control tool. It is assumed that eight weeks of the project have passed. The clear bars (identical to those in Figure 2.2) have been partially filled in to indicate the progress that has been made against the plan.

One of the shortcomings of the bar chart was the difficulty of determining from it the progress of a project when a bar represented a long period of time. The milestone chart helped overcome this deficiency by breaking up bars into shorter periods of time, each of

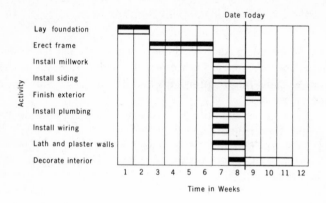

Figure 2.3

which represented the accomplishment of a significant component, or an event, in the long-term job for which the entire bar was labeled. In practice, the more important sections of the milestone chart became numbered as events, and these numbers were explained in a key when the milestone blocks were not drawn large enough to accommodate information within themselves. A bar chart subsequently made into a milestone chart is shown in Figures 2.4 and 2.5.

While the milestone charts constituted something of an improvement over bar charts, they inherited the other major deficiency

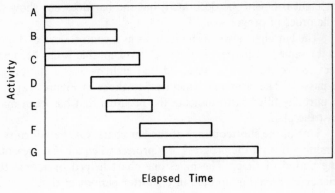

Figure 2.4

of their predecessors, that of failing to show interdependencies between bars or milestones. Only one additional feature was necessary in order to show interrelationships and dependencies—arrows connecting milestones.

Thus, in the evolutionary process, milestones became events and arrows represented activities. The result was a network. The milestone chart of Figure 2.5 is shown as a network in Figure 2.6. The network technique makes clear the interrelationships of all activities and events.

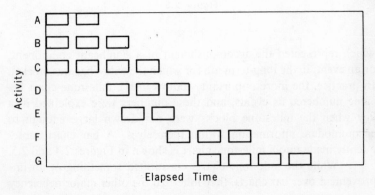

Figure 2.5

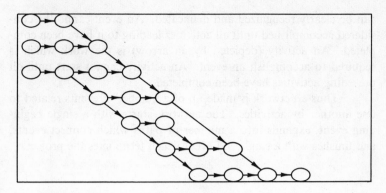

Figure 2.6

2.5 THE NETWORK

The network is the basic PERT device; it is a pictorial representation of the interrelationships of all required events and activities that comprise a project. Events and activities are the two basic components of the network. Figure 2.7 is an example.

An event (depicted by an ellipse) is a specific instant of time; therefore an event cannot consume time. An event can be either the start or the end of a mental or physical task, a point in time which

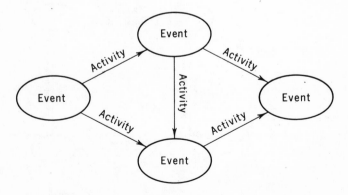

Figure 2.7

can be clearly recognized and delineated. An event cannot be considered accomplished until all activities leading to it have been completed. An activity (depicted by an arrow) is the work which is required to accomplish an event. An activity cannot start until all preceding activities have been completed.

Thus a network is made up of a number of events related to one another by activities. The network starts with a single beginning event, expands into a number of paths which connect events, and finishes with a single end event which terminates the project.

2.6   ORIENTATION AND NOMENCLATURE

The designer of a network could emphasize either the events or the activities. With PERT it is the event which is stressed.

An activity-oriented network is one in which identifications and descriptions are those of activities that must be accomplished between events. Figure 2.8 is a section of an activity-oriented network.

An event-oriented network is one in which the identifications and descriptions are those of events that take place during the project rather than those of activities that must be accomplished in order for the events to occur. Figure 2.9 is a section of an event-oriented net-

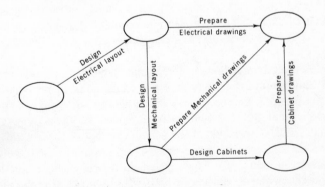

Figure 2.8

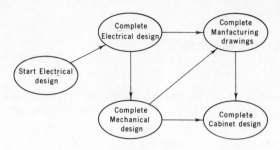

Figure 2.9

work. It can be seen that the activities that take place between events are not defined.

Since PERT is an event-oriented technique, interest is focused upon the start or completion of events rather than on the activities themselves. Thus it is important that events be clearly described. Two rules should be observed in writing events into the network bubbles.

1.   Every bubble should begin with the word *start* or *complete*. Since an event is the beginning or end of an activity and can consume no time, all bubbles on the network stand for either the start or completion of some activity. In practice, the words *start* and *complete* are shortened to *S* and *C*.

2.   The remainder of the words (usually two to four) written into the event bubble should be succinct and descriptive. Usually a noun (the thing worked on) is the main word and the modifying descriptive words are either adjectives or some verb form (gerunds, participles) that will give a clear description. Examples of events might be *S prestressed roof*, *C poured foundation*, or *C hiring shipping clerks*.

The descriptive words written into an event bubble are usually vitally important at the beginning of a project. Everyone concerned must understand and be reminded at a glance what kind of roof is planned, what kind of foundation is called for, what clerks are needed. In later revisions of the network, many of these words can be omitted if all persons concerned are well acquainted with the facts and ideas they conveyed. This is particularly true of events that have transpired by the time later network revisions call for redrawing. The event wording then could be shortened simply to *C roof*, *C foundation*, or *C hiring*.

2.7   SKELETON NETWORKS

It would be an inordinately complex task for a PERT analyst or a team of analysts to draw at first try a detailed network for even a mildly complicated project. (A network illustrating the building and equipping of a new plant may have 1500 activities and 1000 events, the drawing for which would fill up an entire office wall.) This difficulty is avoided through the use of a skeleton network which depicts the main parts of the project from start to end event but lacks the completeness of a detailed network. The purpose of the skeleton network is to display the logic of the total project and to expand the detail of the project beyond the bar chart. Figure 2.10 is a skeleton network designed from the bar chart depicted in Figure 2.2.

2.8   DESIGNING AND DRAWING THE NETWORK

As we pointed out earlier, the final objective of a project must be clearly stated before the network is drawn. This objective then becomes the end event of the network. From the bar chart or other preliminary information a skeleton network must first be drawn, the purpose being to insure the logic of the relationships and sequences of the work required for the project. In preparing this first network, it is common practice to begin with the end event in the project and work backward.

The reason for working backward is that many analysts find it easier to think of work that precedes an activity than to think of the work that follows. It is also normal practice to follow a single path of activities back to the start rather than alternately to pursue several paths, each for only a few activities. The single path method seems to speed the process and minimize errors. Experience has shown that the best path to trace backward initially is one involving physical activities (buildings, equipment) rather than one involving more abstract activities (training, designing, ordering). It appears that visualization enhances network diagraming.

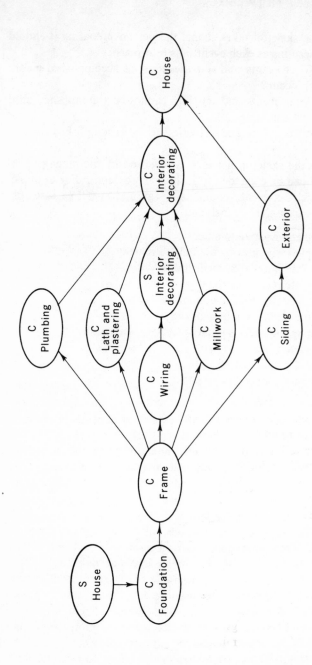

Figure 2.10 (SOURCE: K. L. Dean, "Fundamentals of Network Planning and Analysis," Remington Rand Univac Division, January, 1962)

As the skeleton takes shape, the person preparing it should ask three questions as each event falls into place:

1.   What events and activities must be accomplished before this event can occur?

2.   What events and activities cannot be accomplished until after this event is completed?

3.   What events and activities can be accomplished concurrently?

After the skeleton network is reviewed by the managers responsible, it can be expanded to include more detail. For example, the single skeleton event "complete design and install #3 assembly line" may be expanded to include:

Complete design equipment
Complete engineering committee review
Complete purchase specifications
Complete receive supplier proposals
Complete engineering committee review
Complete place equipment orders
Complete supplier submits factory specifications
Complete design review
Complete factory tests
Complete deliver equipment
Complete install equipment

The amount of detail in the expanded network depends on several factors:

1.   The degree to which critical activities can be identified.

2.   The apparent ease or difficulty of controlling these critical activities.

3.   The amount of time allowed by the project schedule relative to the amount of time required.

4.   The level to which responsibility for various phases of the project is delegated throughout management.

5.   The extent to which information is available.

Generally speaking, it is desirable to diagram activities to be accomplished in the near future in more detail than those to be performed six or more months later. Also, activities likely to make up the longest critical path should be diagramed in more detail than those likely to have more than sufficient available time.

The length of an activity arrow need bear no relationship to the length of time needed to complete the activity. If activity arrows could be drawn proportionate to time, that information would probably be useful to management. Experience has shown, however, that it is impractical to try to do so. It is a difficult enough task to draw initial networks logically correct without detailed regard for time. Furthermore, networks are dynamic and changing frequently, and a change in even a single activity time may affect many others on the same network.

Arrow length ≠ time.

Drawing event bubbles in different shapes, as shown in Figure 2.11, is often helpful in making possible faster identification of

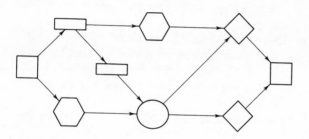

Figure 2.11

responsibilities. One of many criteria can be used for the utilization of different shapes of bubbles:

1. Personnel responsibility (Smith, Jones, Black).
2. Function (production, sales, finance).
3. Organizational responsibility (architect, consultant, supplier, own organization).

or any of several other possibilities. The denotation of different bubbles' shapes can be explained in a simple key in one corner of the network sheet.

2.9 TIME ESTIMATES

Once the logic and detail of the network have been established, time estimates must be assigned to each activity. Although single time estimates can be used, three time values for each activity are usually employed:

1.   Optimistic Time (t_o): the length of time required if no complications or unforeseen difficulties arise in performing the activity. In most instances the probability of realizing this time estimate is slight. A rule of thumb is that there should be only one chance in a hundred of accomplishing the activity in less than optimistic time.

2.   Most Likely Time (t_m): the length of time in which the activity is most likely to be completed. This estimate should take into consideration normal circumstances, making allowances for some unforeseen delays, and should be based upon the best information available.

3.   Pessimistic Time (t_p): the length of time required if unusual complications or unforeseen difficulties arise in carrying out the activity. A rule of thumb is that there should be only one chance in a hundred that the activity would require more time than the pessimistic estimate.

If one time estimate only is used, it should be the most likely time (t_m).

In PERT's original uses in research and development, the value of three time estimates was seldom questioned. They aided in evaluating the uncertainty associated with research and development and they provided means of determining statistically the probability of meeting project schedule dates.[2]

Today PERT's extensive use in other types of work has provoked some doubt as to the need for three time estimates. For instance, many tasks performed by construction men (bricklayers, painters, electricians) have productivity levels either specifically or tacitly established by union agreements. Little uncertainty exists in such cases.

The single time estimate has the advantages of simplifying both hand and computer calculations and of making possible the completion of the network with less time and money involved in its preparation. In addition, single-time-estimate PERT networks may be prepared with the smaller, more widely available computers, whereas three-time-estimate networks require large-capacity computers.

---

[2] Probability is discussed in Chapter 3.

It is customary to express time estimates in weeks and decimal fractions thereof. Time estimates are written directly on the network diagram in the t_o–t_m–t_p order and later transferred to separate worksheets. This assures a clearer understanding of the activities involved and reduces the likelihood that an activity will be overlooked (see Figure 2.12).

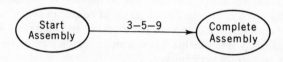

Figure 2.12

The need for useful time estimates is underscored by the following amusing and not atypical experience quoted from an address given by Ernest O. Codier of the General Electric Company.[3]

There is a traditional man/manager gaming model for time estimating. This game runs approximately as follows: you pick up the phone and with casual and disarming friendliness inquire, "Say, George, just off the top of your head, how long will it take to get out 14 frabastats?" Now George is a very competent fellow and he knows instinctively that it would take eight weeks to fabricate 14 frabastats provided everything happened the way it *should* happen. But he does not give you this answer immediately because he has to stop and figure this thing out. In the first place he knows that there will be some normal amount of unforeseen difficulty involved, and he will add a factor to take into account this average uncertainty, say, two weeks. Now he has ten weeks. But George is not misled by the informality of your request; he knows that ultimately in one form or another this is going to show up as a commitment to you, to provide 14 frabastats in a specified time. Furthermore, George knows the nature of the business, and he knows you. He knows that time estimates are traditionally too long, and that somewhere along the line he can expect to get cut back. So at this point, he adds the fat, which is his considered opinion as to how severely this time estimate will get cut later on—say three weeks. He has now arrived at 13 weeks, and this is the figure *you* get. When this proves to be too long, as it invariably does, since it *is in*

[3] *PERT Application at Light Military Electronics Department*, General Electric Company, American Management Association Briefing Session on New Techniques for Management Control. Saranac Lake, N.Y., July 17–19, 1961.

fact too long, the time will get cut as George expects. By one or another mechanism you will work the problem backwards and ask for performance two and a half weeks sooner. You have done pretty well as a manager, and have cut out only approximately the amount that George anticipated; he makes routine grumbling noises, because this is proper form, and $10\frac{1}{2}$ weeks becomes his commitment. Now precisely what do you *know* at this point? Not very much. You do *not* know how long the job should take under ideal circumstances, and you have no measure of potential trouble sources which you as George's manager might be able to help him smooth out. Furthermore, if George actually delivers 14 frabastats in $10\frac{1}{2}$ weeks, you are not really sure whether this was an outstanding effort, or whether it was just an average performance. . . .

Now, let's take a somewhat more aggravated case. The frabastats are an absolutely vital portion of a crash program related to a missile shoot that must occur on such-and-such a date. You're pretty sure George can do better than he is doing. In all managerial honesty you have got to see that this thing is done faster and you need to impress George with this necessity. So under these circumstances you cut George's time more heavily. This is known as setting a challenging goal. "Look, George, we have a tough one this time; you've got to cut this program in half—seven weeks is all you can have." George sees immediately that he is below the irreducible minimum of the basic requirements for the job and he screams, "But there is not a chance in a hundred that I can do it that fast."

So George is afraid for his life; he works really hard, and ends up delivering your frabastats in $8\frac{1}{2}$ weeks. This, on its merits, is really an outstanding performance, but is still a week and a half later than you had required. At this point you as the manager have Hobson's choice. You *suspect* that this was a good job, but can't commend George because he didn't deliver as ordered. If you chastise him too harshly, he will get disgusted at being reprimanded for good performance and leave the Company, and you don't want to risk this. On the other hand, if you let him get away with it, he will recognize that your orders are subject to interpretation and that he merely needs to increase his fat-factor. At this point, everybody in the gaming model has to readjust his coefficients. This is a hell of a way to run a business.

Unfortunately, this *is* a well established way of playing the game, but it is *not* securing the results we need. To meet the requirements of the massive engineering situation operating in today's technology, we need a *new* game with *new* rules. PERT is the game.

2.10   GATHERING TIME ESTIMATES

Time estimates should be gathered by the PERT planner from the persons who have the responsibilities for doing the work the activities represent. Most frequently these are engineers, although many others such as equipment manufacturers, architects, contractors, line managers, and training directors also contribute times.

Solicitation of time estimates is currently the subject of research. Although a number of PERT practitioners have decided preferences for one or another method of soliciting times, no method is generally accepted. It has been observed that time estimates may vary depending, among other things, upon:

1.   The order in which times are solicited (optimistic, most likely, pessimistic).

2.   The relative ranks of the solicitor and PERT analyst (peer, superior, subordinate).

3.   The job of the estimator (engineer, R & D, production, sales).

4.   The likelihood that times are critical.

5.   The quality of recent estimates.

An experienced PERT analyst might observe that:

Experience has shown the optimistic time estimate is the easiest to get. This represents the time the activity would take if everything went almost perfectly. Next to be solicited should be the pessimistic time, or the time that would be necessary if almost everything possible went wrong. This one-two question sequence puts the time estimators in the position of having first to identify and examine all the things that would have to go right and then to determine how much time would be added if these things failed to operate smoothly. Then the most likely time, or time that would be required if everything occurred as it normally does, should be solicited. It also avoids balanced time estimates such as 3, 4, and 5 weeks, or 2, 4, and 6 weeks, which usually indicate that the estimators are giving insufficient thought to time requirements.

Times usually are solicited through interviews, that is, orally, rather than by written communication. Time estimates should be obtained by skipping around the network rather than following a specific path. If estimates are obtained by following one path, there is a tendency for the person contributing the times to add them mentally and compare them with a previously conceived notion of the time of the total path. When this occurs and the times being added differ from the preconceived times, the estimator may begin consciously or unconsciously to build in a "fudge" factor to make the two estimates more nearly equal. Skipping around through the network helps assure that each activity is considered fully and independently on its own merits.

Much of the time used in construction of the detailed PERT network is spent determining the proper approach to particular phases of the project. Network design, analysis, and revision consumes 80 to 90 percent of the time expended in the planning phase of PERT. The first completed network typically represents the "all normal" method of operating with standard-size crews, little or no overtime, and all material available when needed. For example, if electricians normally work in teams of two on a 35-hour week on one shift per day, the network should reflect this condition. If an equipment manufacturer promises 60-week delivery (even when you know that under pressure he will give 40-week delivery), 60 weeks should be reflected on the network. If the firm normally has four draftsmen, only the time of four should be shown on the network, even though in all probability several more will be hired. PERT is a dynamic tool, and, as is described below, changes can be made in the network by management to reflect desirable deviations from the "all normal" start.

Furthermore, it is eminently desirable to record, usually on the network itself, all conditions which may be abnormal or misunderstood by users of the network. Thus if an activity time is later shortened because electricians are working two shifts, this abnormal condition, along with the name of the manager authorizing the two shifts, should be recorded on the network.

This technique is shown in Figure 2.13, in which the activity

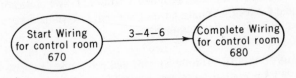

Figure 2.13

in question is identified by the numbers on the two events. A note would also appear on the section of the network diagram sheet reserved for that purpose to this effect: "Activity 670-680 assumes two-shift operation by four-man crews. Authorized 4-12-63 by J. W."

2.11 EVENT NUMBERING

Events should be numbered sequentially when the network is *Order* complete and before it is prepared either for hand or for computer processing. Numbering serves several important purposes. Most *Identifier* important, it makes location and identification of both events and activities possible, since each event becomes known by its number (10, 50, 140) and each activity by the combination of numbers of the events at its start and completion (10-20, 50-70, 140-150).

Another important advantage of sequential numbering is that it aids in the detection of network loops which, while not common in small networks, can become time-wasting pitfalls in large, complex ones. As the name indicates, a loop is a circular path that may lead from one event to another, then another, and so on until it comes back to the first, thus giving a merry-go-round effect. When numbering begins at the start event and proceeds in levels sequentially across the network, as shown in Figure 2.14, each successor event is assigned a higher number than its predecessors. Thus loops can be easily detected since any activity with a higher number at the tail of the arrow than at the head (50-40 or 120-110) would show a possible loop.

A skip-numbering system, as shown in Figure 2.14, permits the addition of events without introducing out-of-sequence numbers. A typical method is to use only every tenth number in the initial coding of the network, such as 10, 20, 30, 40, and so on throughout. Any event added later would be assigned a number between its immediate predecessor and immediate successor events. For instance, in Figure 2.14, if an event were added between events 10 and 20, its number would probably be 15; if two events were added, they might be numbered 13 and 17. If an event were added between events 40 and 100, which are connected in this case by a single activity arrow, the number should be something midway between the predecessor (40)

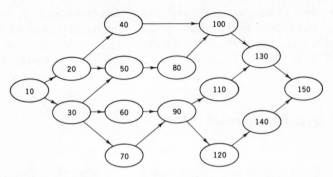

Figure 2.14

and successor (100) events. The numbers 50, 60, 70, 80, and 90 would have to be avoided since they are already in use. Probably 71 would be chosen.

It is best to number the network after obtaining time estimates because experience has shown that persons who provide time estimates often recommend revisions in the network logic. An alternative procedure is to assign numbers immediately upon completion of the network.

2.12 DUMMIES AND LEAD TIMES

The PERT network has been defined as a graphic representation of a project. The network itself is a picture of the work to be done and the events to be accomplished. To keep the network as accurate and descriptive as possible, two devices to maintain its logic are sometimes employed. These are the dummy activity and lead time.

A dummy activity represents no work or expenditure, but is inserted to help maintain the logic of the network. It is easily identifiable because the three time estimates running along its arrow read 0–0–0. The need for dummies arises partly out of the need for showing proper relationships, but largely out of the manner in which network labeling has evolved. It was pointed out in an earlier section of this chapter that every event bubble must be identified *start something* or *complete something*, with the initial verbs usually abbreviated to *S* or *C*. In practice the *S* bubbles are largely eliminated, it being perfectly obvious that anything completed had naturally been started sometime before. By definition, any predecessor event must be completed before a successor event can start and, also by definition, an event consumes no time. Therefore the start of any activity that is not represented by a start bubble is that point in time which follows immediately upon the completion of the predecessor event. Usually it is not necessary to show both of these instantaneous points in time. Current practice favors the use of *complete* events. For instance, notice the network in Figure 2.15.

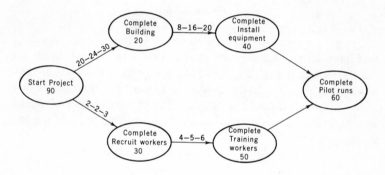

Figure 2.15

What work is represented by activities 40-60 and 50-60? Both arrows represent the same activity, namely, *conduct pilot runs*. This situation occurs any time a *C* bubble is preceded by two or more activity arrows. The time of the activity in question, in this case *conduct pilot runs*, could be recorded on each activity arrow. This approach is rejected by most PERT analysts on the grounds of not being a true description of project tasks and of allowing confusing time duplications to occur on the network. The issue can be resolved by the use of dummy activities as in Figure 2.16. Figure 2.17 shows an alternative method. In both networks it is assumed that workers must be trained and equipment installed before pilot runs can start.

Lead times are assigned to dummy activities in order that project activities will have desired time relationships. Return now

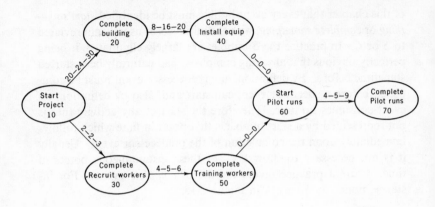

Figure 2.16

to Figure 2.16. Two separate paths must be completed before the
pilot runs can begin. The most likely time of activity 10-20 is 24
weeks, and that of activity 20-40 is 16 weeks. The most likely time
of activity 10-30 is only 2 weeks, and that of activity 30-50, 5 weeks.
In tabular form this relationship of the most likely times of the two
paths is:

Path	Time
10-20-40	$24 + 16 = 40$ weeks
10-30-50	$2 + 5 = 7$ weeks

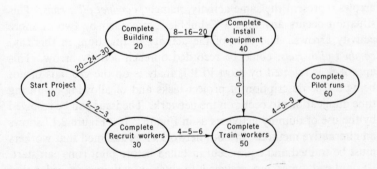

Figure 2.17

It is quite unlikely that workers will be recruited and trained at the beginning of the project and left idle for 33 weeks waiting for the building and equipment to be completed. It is much more reasonable to expect that they will be recruited and trained at about the time they are needed. How can this be shown on the network? A lead time dummy to handle this case is shown in Figure 2.18.

The calculation of lead time can be handled in different ways, two of which are shown below. Both involve first totaling the time estimates along both paths. This is done as follows:

Totaling the Paths			
Path	Optimistic	Most Likely	Pessimistic
10-30	2	2	3
30-50	4	5	6
	6	7	9
10-20	20	24	30
20-40	8	16	20
	28	40	50

The next step is to subtract the totals of the optimistic, most likely, and pessimistic times of the shorter path from the corresponding figures of the longer path.

Subtracting the Totals			
Path	Optimistic	Most Likely	Pessimistic
10-30-40	28	40	50
25-30-50	6	7	9
	22	33	41

This is written as LT 22-33-41, as shown in Figure 2.18.

An alternative method after the paths have been totaled is slightly simpler. It is to subtract the total of the pessimistic times of the shorter path (9 in this case) from the optimistic times of the

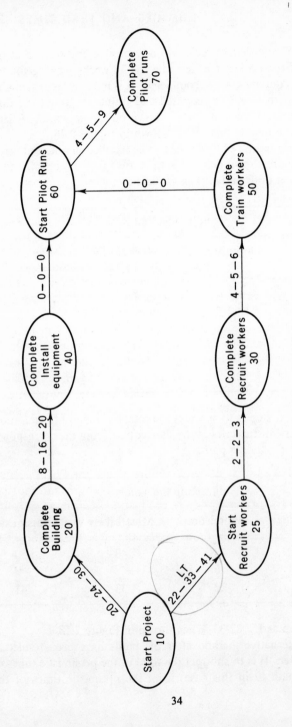

Figure 2.18

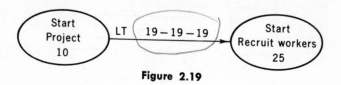

Figure 2.19

longer path (28). The resulting number, 19, is inserted on the activity arrow 10-25 as shown in Figure 2.19.

Actually, the exact amount of lead time indicated is of minor importance because network paths containing lead times which are used for the reasons given in this example are not paths for which time is critical. If the paths were at all critical, lead times would not be used. A second reason for the unimportance of the precision of lead times is that projects are periodically reviewed, making scrutiny and revision of lead times possible as necessary.

There are occasions when assigned lead times can be quite important. Consider a project in which a concrete column is required to support heavy steel beams. In such a case an amount of cure time may be specified to allow the concrete to gain full strength. This would be accomplished on the PERT network by inserting a lead time dummy activity between the two events *complete poured concrete* and *start erecting steel beams* as shown in Figure 2.20.

Another use of lead times can best be understood by returning to the bar chart. See Figure 2.21.

In drawing a network from the bar chart, the PERT analyst must indicate that the three activities (*design, fabricate,* and *test*) can run concurrently for the most part, but that *fabricate* must start two weeks later than *design* and *test* must start two weeks later than *fabricate*. There are two methods for handling this, the first of which

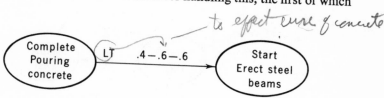

Figure 2.20

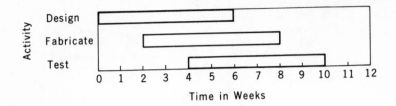

Figure 2.21

employs lead times as in Figure 2.22. An alternative method of drawing the network is shown in Figure 2.23. This method uses dummies but not lead times. This network is dependent upon the possibility of finding definable break points in activities so that long activities can be broken into segments. Advocates of the method shown in Figure 2.23 prefer it because it has no lead time. Advocates of the method employed in Figure 2.22 favor it because it requires fewer events and activities.

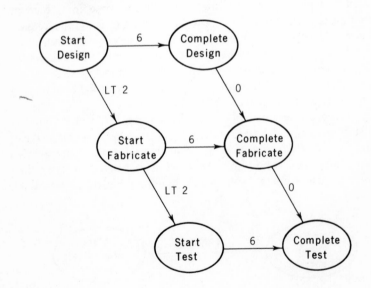

Figure 2.22

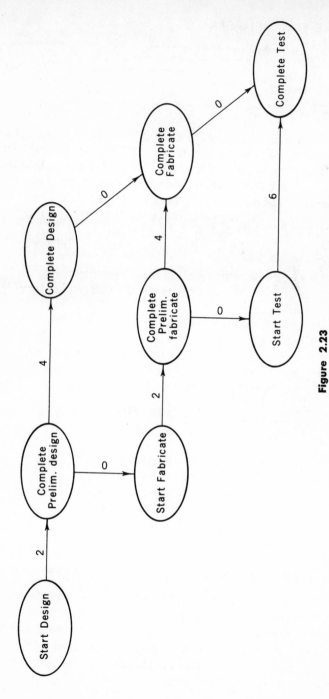

Figure 2.23

37

2.13 SUMMARY

In order to attain any objective, it is necessary to plan. The more complex the project the more necessary is good planning. Because of its demonstrated superiority over predecessor techniques, PERT has experienced rapid and widespread acceptance by business management. The basic planning device is the network, a pictorial representation of the interrelationships of all work that must be accomplished in order to attain a project objective.

In preparing a network the following steps are followed:

1. Get a precise statement of the project objective.
2. Determine the activities required to accomplish the project objective.
3. Draw a skeleton network of the project (often with the aid of a bar chart).
4. Expand the skeleton network to a full-size network.
5. Solicit and record three time estimates for each activity.
6. Number the events in the network.

The exact configuration that any PERT network takes is a function of many variables. These include:

1. The use to which the network will be put.
2. The skill of the PERT analyst.
3. The organizational attitudes regarding dummies and lead times.
4. The availability of information.
5. The amount of schedule slack.
6. The degree to which critical activities can be identified.
7. The point in time at which the network is observed.

Despite the fact that it is unlikely that any two PERT analysts would draw identical networks, this is not to say that the information provided by the two networks would be different. Provided that the analysts were both competent, the information returned by the two networks would probably vary slightly in detail, but would comprise a useful plan of the project at hand.

2.14 QUESTIONS

1. What is a project objective and why is one needed?

2. In what specific ways are milestone charts superior to bar charts? What shortcomings of milestone charts are overcome by networks?

3. Why is it a requirement of the PERT technique that there be only a single beginning event and a single end event?

4. What would be the likely result of the use of inadequate or poorly worded event bubble descriptions?

5. Cite reasons why it is usually desirable to draw a skeleton network from a bar chart.

6. Justify each of the reasons given for the degree of detail in an expanded PERT network.

7. Under what conditions would you prefer to use one rather than three time estimates?

8. List several types of tasks that you feel are compatible with the use of one time estimate; of three time estimates. Be prepared to defend your selections.

9. List some of the factors that are likely to affect the validity of time estimates.

10. What qualifications make a person a good time estimator?

11. What is the primary reason for using a skip-numbering system on PERT networks? A sequential numbering system?

12. Differentiate between dummies and lead times. Describe situations in which each would be used.

2.15 PROBLEMS

1. Are the interpretations that follow the network sections correct?

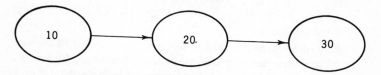

Figure 2.24

Event 20 cannot start until event 10 is completed.
Event 20 cannot start until event 30 is completed. ✗

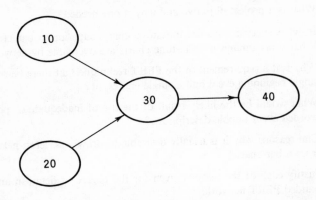

Figure 2.25

Event 30 cannot start until events 10 and 20 are completed. ✓
Event 20 cannot start until event 10 is completed. ✗

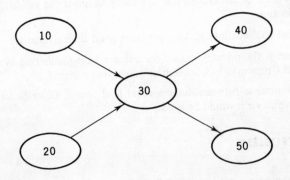

Figure 2.26

Both events 30 and 40 must be completed before event 50 can start. ✗
Event 30 must be completed before either event 40 or 50 can start. ✓
Both events 10 and 20 must be completed before events 40 or 50 can be started.

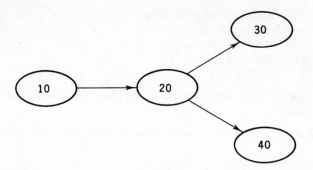

Figure 2.27

Event 30 must be completed before event 40 can start. ✗
Events 30 and 40 must be completed before event 20 can start. ✗
Event 10 must be completed before event 40 can start. ✓

2. A factory maintenance superintendent wishes to rebuild a key machine during the vacation shutdown. The following tasks must be accomplished:

1. Move machine to repair shop.
2. Order replacement parts.
3. Remove old machine foundation.
4. Repair machine parts.
5. Reassemble machine.
6. Build new machine foundation.
7. Move machine parts to factory.
8. Dismantle machine.

Draw a PERT network showing how these tasks would be accomplished.

3. A newly promoted executive has received authorization to spruce up his office. He has prepared the following list of tasks to be accomplished:

1. Install new carpeting.
2. Install air conditioning.
3. Clean up office.
4. Remove furnishings (equipment and drapes).
5. Order new equipment.
6. Install new equipment.
7. Paint office.

8. Install new electrical fixtures.
9. Wash windows.
10. Order new carpeting.
11. Order new drapes.
12. Install drapes.

Draw a PERT network showing how these tasks would be accomplished.

4. Draw a PERT network based on the following bar chart.

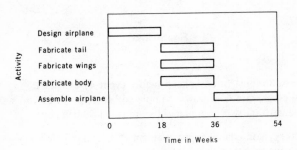

Figure 2.28

5. Draw a PERT network based on Figure 2.29. Assume 4 weeks to each month.

6. Draw a bar chart depicting the manner in which you would accomplish one of the following:

1. Paint your home.
2. Make a dress.
3. Remove, grease, and replace the rear wheel of a bicycle.
4. Prepare for a formal dinner.
5. Overhaul the engine of your car.
6. Build a model airplane.

Your objective is to complete the task in the fastest possible time. Assume that you can have as many competent assistants as you require.

7. Draw a PERT network from the bar chart you drew in answer to the foregoing question.

8. Draw a bar chart depicting the manner in which you would accomplish one of the following:

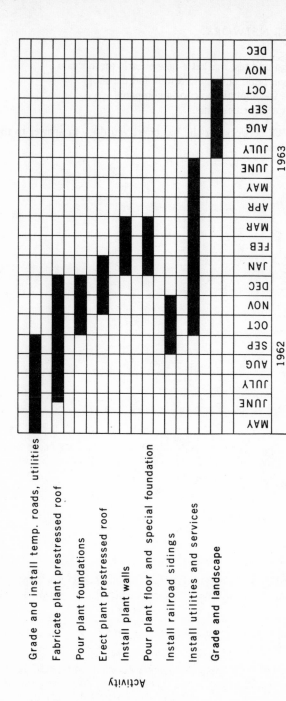

Figure 2.29

43

     1. Design and test market a new electric toothbrush.

     2. Design, build and equip a tool and die shop.

     3. Close the annual books of a company.

     4. Float a securities issue.

9. Draw a PERT network for the bar chart you drew in answer to the foregoing question.

3 ▸   COMPUTATIONAL PROCEDURE

3.1   OVERVIEW

Up to this point the discussion has been centered on what PERT is, what its potentialities are, and how a network is set up. Now we can turn to the problem of how to determine the time required by the various paths through the network and the likelihood of meeting scheduled dates.

The procedure during the computation stage is, first, to convert the three time estimates for each activity to a single time estimate; next, to trace through each path to establish the earliest expected time of each event; then, to reverse steps and trace back the several paths to determine the latest allowable date for each event; and, finally, to determine the all-important slack. The likelihood of meeting the completion schedule can then be determined through the use of a statistical technique employing the normal curve.

Slack is the difference in time between the scheduled completion date of the entire project and the length of any path. For any project not having a scheduled completion date, the date of the final

Slack ± *(margin annotation)*

event on the longest path is taken to be the completion date. Slack can be either positive or negative. The term "slack" should not be taken to mean that there is time to spare. If a path is longer in weeks than the time allowed for the entire project (as in the case of a path 34 weeks long in a project for which only 32 weeks have been allowed), the slack would be negative (in this case, −2). If the path is shorter in weeks than the time allowed for the project, the slack is positive.

3.2   INFORMATION GAINED FROM CALCULATIONS

Once the PERT network is drawn and time estimates are solicited and recorded on the network, management has a plan which describes in detail the logical sequence of events that must be completed in order to attain the project objective. But that is just the beginning. With a few calculations, management can quickly have the following:

1.   The amount of time that each activity is likely to consume.

2.   The earliest time by which each event can be expected to take place.

3.   The latest time by which each event can be completed if it is not to cause delay in meeting the scheduled termination date of the total job.

4.   The amount of slack, positive or negative, between the time each event is scheduled to be completed and the time allowed by the project termination date.

5.   Identification of the critical (longest), the semicritical (shorter), and the slack (shortest) paths through the network, and the amount of slack, positive or negative, in each.

6.   The probability of meeting the scheduled time of the project completion.

7.   A basis for the systematic analysis and revision of the project to meet project objectives. This is explained in Chapter 4.

3.3 DATA NEEDED

Before manual calculations can be begun, the following types of information which have been described in Chapters 1 and 2 must be on hand:

1. A network, graphically presenting the entire project.

2. Activities, the work which is required to accomplish the various tasks which make up the project.

3. Events, the identifying points of the network which do not themselves consume time, but show the beginnings or completions of expected activities.

4. Event identification numbers sequentially arranged.

5. Optimistic, pessimistic, and most likely time estimates for each activity.

Figure 3.1 is a network including all the data mentioned above as necessary.

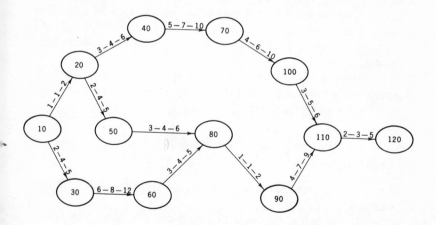

Figure 3.1

3.4   EXPECTED TIME

In order to carry out PERT calculations, it is necessary to know how much time (always measured in weeks) each activity is expected to take. Which of the time estimates (pessimistic, most likely, or optimistic) should be used? Consider the network in Figure 3.1. Two paths through the network are of approximately the same length.

	Pessimistic	Most Likely	Optimistic
Path A: 10-20-40-70-100-110-120	39	26	18
Path B: 10-30-60-80-90-110-120	38	27	18

If the pessimistic times were used, Path A would be the critical path. If most likely times were used, Path B would be the critical path. If optimistic times were used, both paths would be equally critical.

The best estimate to use is a weighted average of all three times, giving the expected time (t_E). This expected time is calculated with the following formula:

$$t_E = \frac{t_o + 4t_m + t_p}{6}$$

in which t_o = optimistic time, t_m = most likely time, and t_p = pessimistic time.

This formula was devised by early users of PERT who recognized the need for t_E, a weighted average of the three time estimates. Their method was to plot the three time estimates as a probability distribution which would occur if the activity it represented were to recur a large number of times. Activity 30-60 from Figure 3.1 is plotted in Figure 3.2.

It was felt that the peak of the distribution would be the most likely time. The peak of the curve in Figure 3.2 is the highest point

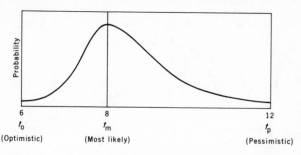

Figure 3.2, *Activity 30-60 from Fig. 3.1*

on the probability scale. Since the likelihood of either the optimistic or pessimistic time's occurring is about 1 in 100, both are located low on the probability scale.— *Namely 101*

Early users of PERT noted a similarity between the distribution in Figure 3.2 and another known to mathematicians as the beta distribution. The parameters of the beta distribution are in one respect different from the parameters of the distributions of PERT times. Nonetheless, it was decided that the similarity was great enough to permit the use of the beta distribution as the model for three-time-estimate PERT.[1]

The calculation of the expected time of an activity through the beta distribution analysis requires mathematical sophistication beyond the level of most college students. Even experts find such calculations tedious. After empirical investigation, mathematicians found that the simple equation above gives results that approximate those gained through rigorous analysis of the beta distribution. Since the distribution of the three time estimates is only an approximation of the beta distribution, it was felt that this further simplification would introduce no significant error. Therefore, this formula has become the standard equation for the calculation of the expected time of an activity.[2]

---

[1] For further discussion on the use of the beta distribution as a model for PERT times, see *Operations Research*, Vol. 10, May–June, 1962, pp. 405–406; and *Institute of Radio Engineers, Transactions on Engineering Management*, Vol. EM-9, September, 1962, pp. 101–102.

[2] For a detailed explanation of the application of the beta distribution and the

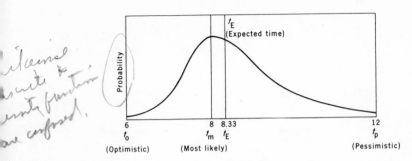

Figure 3.3

In calculating t_E for activity 30-60 of the network in Figure 3.1, the standard equation would be applied as follows:

$$t_E = \frac{t_o + 4t_m + t_p}{6}$$

$$t_E = \frac{6 + 4(8) + 12}{6}$$

$$t_E = 8.33$$

Next, t_E can be placed on the distribution of activity 30-60 which is redrawn in Figure 3.3.

The expected time (t_E) is the weighted average we have been seeking. It divides the area under the curve into two equal parts. There is a 50-50 chance that the activity will require more or less than the expected time.

It is important to note that our formula for t_E will cut the area under the curve into equal parts regardless of any unusual time estimates we may get. Consider the activity in Figure 3.4, which

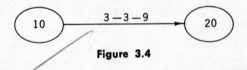

Figure 3.4

derivation of the expected time formula, see *PERT Program Evaluation Research Task Summary Report Phase I*, Special Projects Office, Bureau of Naval Weapons, Department of the Navy, July, 1958, especially Chapter II and Appendix B.

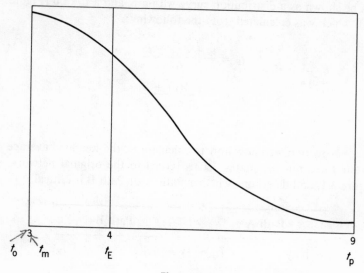

Figure 3.5

can be shown to have a t_E of 4 in the distribution curve of Figure 3.5, which was calculated from the following:

$$t_E = \frac{t_o + 4t_m + t_p}{6}$$

$$t_E = \frac{3 + 4(3) + 9}{6}$$

$$t_E = 4$$

In one set of circumstances, t_m and t_E will be equal. This occurs when balanced time estimates are given, as in Figure 3.6. It

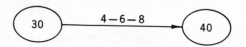

Figure 3.6

can be shown as a distribution curve with a t_E and a t_m of 6 (Figure 3.7), which was calculated from the following:

$$t_E = \frac{t_o + 4t_m = t_p}{6}$$

$$t_E = \frac{4 + 4(6) + 8}{6}$$

$$t_E = 6$$

Now that we know how to calculate t_E, the weighted average of our three time estimates, let us return to the original network, Figure 3.1, and determine whether Path A or Path B is critical.

Path A		Path B	
Activity	$(t_E)^a$	Activity	(t_E)
10-20	1.2	10-30	3.8
20-40	4.2	30-60	8.3
40-70	7.2	60-80	4.0
70-100	6.3	80-90	1.2
100-110	4.8	90-110	6.8
110-120	3.2	110-120	3.2
	26.9		27.3

[a] There are a number of suggested methods for easing the calculation of t_E, including the use of reciprocals and a special slide rule. The author finds it easiest to mentally multiply t_m by 4, add the extremes, and divide by 6.

Path B is thus the critical path. By this fiat.

3.5   EARLIEST EXPECTED TIME = Capital $T_E = \sum_{Path} t_E$

The skills we have developed to this point permit us to determine the critical path on small networks which have few interrelationships. We can also readily calculate the slack in the several paths of simple networks. However, when networks are comprised of more

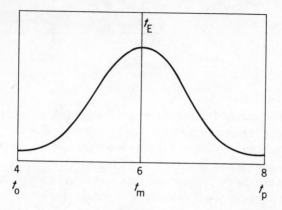

Figure 3.7

than 12 or 15 activities or when two or more activities precede or follow an event, complex relationships can arise. (See Figure 3.8.) This entirely normal occurrence makes it extremely difficult to calculate critical path time and slack without a systematic procedure. Two additional concepts are necessary for use in the calculations procedure—earliest expected time (T_E) and latest allowable time (T_L). In the remainder of this section we will describe the earliest expected time.

The earliest expected time (T_E) refers to the time when an *Capital* T_E event can be expected to be completed. T_E for any event is the total of all the expected times (t_E) of all the activities that precede it.[3] Thus in Figure 3.9 the T_E for event 20 is 3.2 weeks; for event 30, 15.7 weeks (3.2 + 12.5); and for event 40, 24.0 weeks (3.2 + 12.5 + 8.3).

It should be noted that t_E refers to an activity, and that T_E

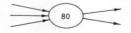

Figure 3.8

---

[3] By this point the reader should recognize t_E as the symbol for expected time. It is our practice to omit description after it has been used several times in conjunction with symbolic notation.

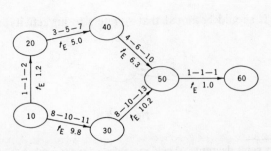

Figure 3.9

refers to an event. The t_E for any activity for which three time estimates are given can be calculated independently. The T_E for a particular event can be calculated only when the t_E's for all preceding activities are known.

When an event has more than one activity arrow leading to it, more than one T_E is calculated. Consider Figure 3.10. The T_E for event 50 is calculated by adding the t_E's of all preceding activities.

Path 10-20-40-50	Path 10-30-50
1.2	
5.0	9.8
6.3	10.2
T_E 12.5	20.0

Which T_E should be used? The higher figure should be used because event 50 cannot be achieved until *all* preceding activities are completed. T_E for event 60 is 21.0 (not 13.5) for the same reason.

Figure 3.10

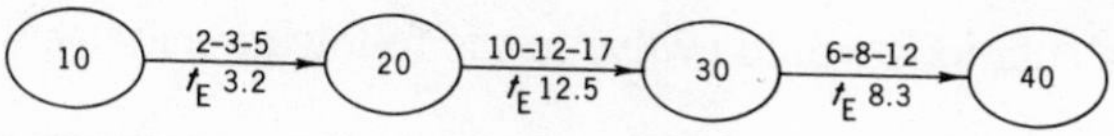

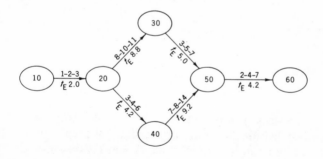

Figure 3.11

3.6 LATEST ALLOWABLE TIME, $T_L = C - \sum_{route} t_E$ or $T_{E,end} - \sum t_E$

The latest allowable time (T_L) refers to the time by which an event must be achieved if the project is to be completed on schedule. If no completion date has been established, the latest allowable time is the T_E for the end event of the project.

The calculation of T_L is accomplished in just the opposite manner from that of T_E. That is, t_E for each activity is progressively subtracted starting from the scheduled completion date (or T_E for the end event if no date has been scheduled) back to any event for which T_L is desired. For example, assume that the project of which Figure 3.11 is a segment must be completed in 45 weeks.

T_L for event 40 is 45 weeks. T_L for event 30 is 45 weeks minus 8.3 weeks, or 36.7 weeks. T_L for event 20 is 24.2 weeks (36.7 − 12.5), and T_L for event 10 is 21 weeks (24.2 − 3.2).[4]

When an event has more than one successor event, more than one T_L will be calculated. Consider Figure 3.12. What is the T_L for event 20 if T_L for event 60 is 22.0 weeks?

Figure 3.12

---

[4] Another way of expressing times is in calendar dates instead of units of time. If the project completion date in this example had been October 25, then T_L for event 40 would have been October 25; for event 30, August 28; for event 20, June 3; and for event 10, May 10.

Calculations would evolve in the following manner:

Path 20-30-50-60		Path 20-40-50-60	
t_E 50-60	4.2	t_E 50-60	4.2
t_E 30-50	5.0	t_E 40-50	9.2
t_E 20-30	8.8	t_E 20-40	4.2
Σt_E	18.0	Σt_E	17.6
T_L event 60	22.0	T_L event 60	22.0
less Σt_E 20-30-50-60	18.0	*less* Σt_E 20-40-50-60	17.6
T_L event 20	4.0	T_L event 20	4.4

If Path 20-30-50-60 is followed back, the T_L for event 20 is 4.0 weeks. If Path 20-40-50-60 is followed back, the T_L for event 20 is 4.4 weeks. Which T_L should be used? The lower figure must be used because event 20 must occur early enough to allow time for *all* succeeding activities to be completed. Selection of the lower figure permits the time necessary for path 20-30-50-60, which consumes more time than path 20-40-50-60.

3.7 SLACK $= T_L - T_E$

The slack of a particular path is the difference between the time scheduled for the entire project and that needed for the path. Now that we know how to calculate T_E and T_L, we can easily calculate slack, the difference between the two. T_L is the time by which an event *must* be achieved if the project is expected to be completed on schedule. T_E is the time at which an event is expected to be achieved.

The slack of a path is positive if the time at which the final event of the path is expected to be achieved occurs earlier than the project completion date. If that time is later than the completion date, the slack is negative. Paths with negative slack become critical paths, the one with the greatest negative figure being *the* critical path (that is, longest and needing most attention).

3.8 REVIEW OF TERMINOLOGY

Before we go on to a systematic method of calculating criticality and slack of network paths, a brief review of terminology is in order.

Term	Description	Referent
t_o	Optimistic time	Activity
t_m	Most likely time	Activity
t_p	Pessimistic time	Activity
t_E	Expected time	Activity
T_E	Earliest expected time	Event
T_L	Latest allowable time	Event
Slack	Project schedule time minus length of path	Path

3.9 COMPUTATIONAL PROCEDURES [5]

All the concepts necessary to determine critical paths and slack have been described in this chapter. The next essential is a systematic routine that will facilitate the skillful use of these concepts. The 21-activity network in Figure 3.13 can serve as an example. It has a scheduled completion time of 45 weeks.

After the network has been laid out, the three time estimates for each activity solicited, and the events numbered sequentially, the

---

[5] There are a number of different computational procedures, all of which give the same result. The method described here most closely conforms to one developed by Booz·Allen & Hamilton, Inc., management consultants.

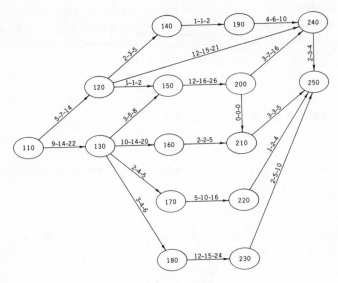

Figure 3.13

analyst can begin to make up a worksheet on which to make calculations.

Table 3.1 is the preliminary worksheet. Notice that it has nine columns. The first five of these (successor event, predecessor event, and the three time-estimate columns) can be filled in simply by recording the information from the network, as has been done in Table 3.1.

The first event recorded on the worksheet is the end event (250, in this case), which is placed at the top of the successor event column. Next, all the events immediately preceding event 250 are recorded in the predecessor event column, beginning with the highest-numbered predecessor on the same line with event 250, and then on down the column until all immediate predecessors of event 250 are listed on separate lines. In this case, four predecessors—240, 230, 220, 210—are listed since these four events are directly connected to event 250 by activity arrows.

The next step is to return to the successor column to list the event numerically next lowest to event 250. Event 240, in this case, would be listed at this time as a successor event, and its three predecessors (found by tracing back the three arrows leading to event 240)

TABLE 3.1

Computation Worksheet

Successor event	Predecessor event	t_o	t_m	t_p	t_E	T_E	T_L	Slack
250	240	2	3	4				
	230	2	5	10				
	220	1	2	4				
	210	3	3	5				
240	200	3	7	16				
	190	4	6	10				
	120	12	15	21				
230	180	12	15	24				
220	170	5	10	16				
210	200	0	0	0				
	160	2	2	5				
200	150	12	16	26				
190	140	1	1	2				
180	130	3	4	6				
170	130	2	4	5				
160	130	10	14	20				
150	130	3	5	8				
	120	1	1	2				
140	120	2	3	5				
130	110	9	14	22				
120	110	5	8	14				

would then be listed in the predecessor event column as described above. The three predecessors of event 240 are 200, 190, and 120.

The third number to appear in the successor event column is the next lowest number numerically of all those on the network. This is not necessarily the second successor event's highest-numbered predecessor. In this case, the third event in the successor column is 230, which is not listed among 240's predecessors at all. In preparing worksheets, it is always important to refer back to the network for successor event numbers rather than to refer to the predecessor event column for this information. Sometimes the numbers will match, but often they will not.

This listing of events and their predecessors should proceed, with successor events in exact reverse numerical order, until the start event of the network is reached. Special care should be taken not to overlook any event numbers that may have been inserted after the network was first numbered. These would have been given intervening numbers and could be missed by a person skipping down the worksheet in backward leaps of 10. There are no such cases in the network at hand, but should there be an event 205 inserted, care should be taken not to miss putting it on the worksheet. Every event on the network, except the very first one, must appear in its proper order in the successor event column of the worksheet. Every event, except the very last one, must appear at least once in the predecessor event column, and many may appear more than once, although in no special numerical order.

After both event columns are filled in and checked for order, the optimistic, most likely, and pessimistic times for each activity are taken from the network and put on the worksheet. On the worksheet in Table 3.1, the first line is for the times of activity 240-250, the second for activity 230-250, the third for activity 220-250, and so on. The tenth line is for activity 200-210, a dummy activity for which the times must be recorded even though they are simply 0–0–0. The last line is for activity 110-120, the first activity of the network. After all these events and activity times are recorded, the worksheet has been properly prepared for calculations.

The first of the columns necessitating calculation is the t_E column (sixth from left). Expected time (t_E) of an activity is calculated as follows:[6]

$$t_E = \frac{t_o + 4t_m + t_p}{6}$$

As was pointed out earlier in this chapter, this formula results in a weighted average showing the time which an activity could be expected to take, according to all information available. While methods of doing this vary, quick mental calculations can be made by multiplying the middle of the three time columns (t_m) by 4, adding the t_o and t_p columns, and dividing by 6. For Table 3.1, the t_E on

---

[6] Some analysts prefer to calculate and record t_E on the network and then transfer only t_E to the worksheet, omitting the transfer of t_o, t_m, and t_p.

the first line (that is, for activity 240-250) would be 3.0; that on the second line (activity 230-250), 5.3; that on the third line (activity 220-250) 2.2; and so on. The t_E column should be followed down until an expected time is calculated for each activity.

Earliest expected time (T_E) to achieve an event is calculated next. It is the sum of the expected times (t_E) of all the activities from the beginning of the network to the event in question. It is assumed for this purpose that all activities start as early as possible. The earliest expected time (T_E) for each event is calculated as follows:

$$T_E \text{ (successor)} = T_E \text{ (predecessor)} + t_E \text{ (activity)}$$

For example, T_E for event 120 is 8.5, the expected time for completion of the activity 110-120. Similarly, T_E for event 160 is 14.5 plus 14.3 (t_E for the activity 130-160), a total of 28.8.

When a successor event has more than one activity arrow leading to it, more than one T_E will be calculated. The greatest should be circled and used in calculating T_E for succeeding activities. For example, T_E for event 150 is 19.7 rather than 9.7. Therefore, T_E for event 200 is 19.7 + 17.0, or 36.7. The purpose of using the greatest number for subsequent calculations is to assure that time enough is allowed for the path consuming the greatest amount of time.

The latest allowable time (T_L) refers to the time by which an event must be completed if the project is to be completed on schedule. T_L for any event is calculated by subtracting from the scheduled length of the project the length of the longest path backward from the end of the network to the event in question. In those instances in which a project does not have a scheduled completion time, the T_E of the end event is also used as T_L for that event.

For example, if the scheduled time for event 250 is 45.0, then the latest allowable time for event 250, designated as T_L in Table 3.1, is 45.0. To calculate the latest allowable time for the predecessors of event 250, the following formula should be used:

$$T_L \text{ (predecessor)} = T_L \text{ (successor)} - t_E \text{ (activity)}$$

Thus for event 240, T_L equals 45.0 (T_L for event 250) minus 3.0 (t_E for the activity 240-250), or 42.0. When an event has two or more succeeding activities, more than one T_L figure will be calculated.

The lowest of these figures should be used. For example, event 200 appears twice in the predecessor event column. For successor event 240, T_L for event 200 is 42.0 − 7.8, which equals 34.2. For successor event 210, T_L for event 200 is 41.7 − 0.0, which equals 41.7. The lower figure, 34.2, should be used since this will assure that time enough is allowed for the path consuming the greatest amount of time.

Determination of slack is mechanically the easiest PERT calculation to make, but conceptually it is difficult to understand. The calculation is as follows:

$$\text{Slack} = T_L - T_E$$

For the first line on the worksheet in Table 3.1 this calculation is:

$$\text{Slack} = 45.0 - 47.5 = -2.5$$

For the second line:

$$\text{Slack} = 45.0 - 40.0 = 5.0$$

A completed worksheet, identical to the one in Table 3.1, but with expected times, earliest expected times, latest allowable times, and slacks filled in, appears in Table 3.2.

The objective of all these calculations is to identify the critical path, the semicritical paths, and the slack paths. All events lying on the same path in the network have identical slack figures on the worksheet. The critical path begins with the start event, terminates with the end event, and lies along those activities which show the identical slack figure which is the lowest positive figure or the greatest negative figure.

In the case of Table 3.2, a negative figure (−2.5) appears in the worksheet. By beginning at the bottom of the slack column of the worksheet and working up to find the first −2.5 slack, the analyst can identify the critical path by jotting down both the predecessor event and successor event on the same line with the first −2.5, then the successor events of each −2.5 slack line on the worksheet. The critical path in this case would be 110-130-150-200-240-250. Figure 3.14 is the sample network of Figure 3.13 redrawn to show the critical path.

TABLE 3.2

Hand Calculation Worksheet*

Successor event	Predecessor event	t_o	t_m	t_p	t_E	T_E	T_L	Slack
250	240	2	3	4	3.0	47.5	45.0	−2.5
	230	2	5	10	5.3	40.0		5.0
	220	1	2	4	2.2	30.7		14.3
	210	3	3	5	3.3	40.0		5.0
240	200	3	7	16	7.8	44.5	42.0	−2.5
	190	4	6	10	6.3	19.2		22.8
	120	12	15	21	15.5	24.0		18.0
230	180	12	15	24	16.0	34.7	39.7	5.0
220	170	5	10	16	10.2	28.5	42.8	14.3
210	200	0	0	0	0	36.7	41.7	5.0
	160	2	2	5	2.5	31.3		10.4
200	150	12	16	26	17.0	36.7	34.2	−2.5
190	140	1	1	2	1.2	12.9	35.7	22.8
180	130	3	4	6	4.2	18.7	23.7	5.0
170	130	2	4	5	3.8	18.3	32.6	14.3
160	130	10	14	20	14.3	28.8	39.2	10.4
150	130	3	5	8	5.2	19.7	17.2	−2.5
	120	1	1	2	1.2	9.7		7.5
140	120	2	3	5	3.2	11.7	34.5	22.8
130	110	9	14	22	14.5	14.5	12.0	−2.5
120	110	5	8	14	8.5	8.5	16.0	7.5

* Bold-face numbers are those which an analyst would encircle as he prepares the worksheet. Each of these is the greatest T_E for an event having more than one predecessor, and would be used in calculating T_E for succeeding activities.

It should be understood that slack affects equally an entire path, not just one activity. For instance, the critical path in Figure 3.14 is shown as 110-130-150-200-240-250. The slack of −2.5 refers to the entire path. Suppose the time for activity 150-200, which is 17 weeks, could be shortened to 14.5 weeks. This would cancel the −2.5 weeks of slack for the *entire path*, so that the slack would become zero.

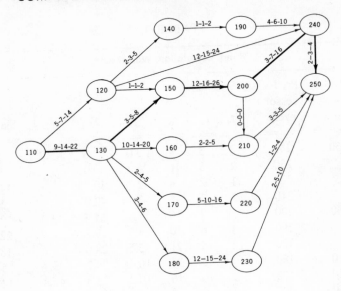

Figure 3.14

Selection of semicritical and slack paths in a network, after the critical path is identified, is a matter of judgment. In Figure 3.14 selection of these paths must depend on arbitrary decisions about time, since nothing else of the project is known.

Semicritical paths in this case are:

Path	Slack
130-180-230-250	5.0
200-210-250	5.0
110-120-150	7.5

Slack paths are:

Path	Slack
130-160-210	10.4
130-170-220-250	14.3
120-240	18.0
120-140-190-240	22.8

3.10   PROBABILITY OF MEETING SCHEDULED DATE

When we needed a value for the time consumed by an activity, we elected to use the value of expected time (t_E) instead of using the pessimistic, optimistic, or most likely time. The expected time was the time which split the probability distribution into equal parts; that is, 50 percent of the area under the beta curve was to the right of t_E and 50 percent was to the left. We said that the expected time had a 50-50 chance of being achieved.

If the expected times of the activities along the longest path in the network (the critical path) were totaled, the figure for the end event would be the earliest expected time (T_E) of the project and would have a 50-50 chance of being met. Another way of saying the same thing is that there is a probability of .5 that the earliest expected time of the project would be achieved.

Usually, however, a project has a scheduled completion date, and it is unlikely that such a date would coincide with the earliest expected time of the end event. In such an instance, the probability of meeting the scheduled date would not be .5. Our task is to determine what it would be.

Experience has shown that the probability distribution of T_E for a project comprised of a number of activities is approximated by the normal distribution. Our approach is to measure the area under the normal curve that represents the amount of time allowed by the scheduled date of the project and compare this area with the total area under the curve. The result is the probability of meeting the scheduled completion date. Figure 3.15 is such a representation of the project for which the calculations in Table 3.2 were made.

The project is scheduled to be completed in 45 weeks (shown by the shaded area under the curve in Figure 3.15. T_E for the last event in the project is 47.5 weeks (shown as the mean). The probability that the project will be completed on time (i.e., in 45 weeks as originally scheduled) is less than .5 and can be calculated statistically.

The first step in preparing for this statistical calculation is to understand and appreciate standard deviation. One standard deviation (σ) from the mean of a normal curve includes 68 percent of the area under the curve. Two standard deviations (2σ) include 95

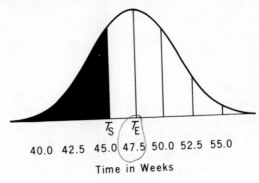

T_S T_E

40.0 42.5 45.0 47.5 50.0 52.5 55.0

Time in Weeks

Figure 3.15

percent of the area. Three standard deviations (3σ) include 99 percent. See Figure 3.16.

The standard deviation is a measure of the spread or range of a probability distribution; a high σ indicates a widespread distribution and a low σ, the opposite.

The σ of T_E for any event is a result of the spread between the sum of the optimistic (t_o) and pessimistic (t_p) time estimates for all preceding activities on the path on which that event is located.

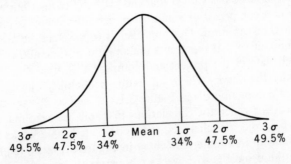

3σ 2σ 1σ Mean 1σ 2σ 3σ
49.5% 47.5% 34%   34%   47.5% 49.5%

$1\sigma = 68\%$

$2\sigma = 95\%$

$3\sigma = 99\%$

Figure 3.16

If there are wide differences between t_o and t_p, the range of the σ will be wide. We will measure the σ from the mean in our example, which is equivalent to saying we will calculate the number of σ's in the difference between the project's scheduled date and the mean. This σ figure can be referred to a table which converts the deviation to a measure of the area beyond the scheduled date. This measure is the probability figure that we are seeking.

The equation for this problem is:

$$\sigma = \frac{T_S - T_E}{\sigma\Sigma\sigma^2}$$ Not correct
a at least not used!

in which:

T_S = scheduled completion time of the project
$\Sigma\sigma^2$ = the sum of the variances of the activities on the path being considered
$\sigma\Sigma\sigma^2$ = the standard deviation of the sum of the variances

Using the data in Figure 3.14 and Table 3.2, we will determine the probability of the project's and event's being completed on schedule. To do so, we need certain data to "plug into" the formula above. T_S, the scheduled date, is given and is 45.0 weeks. T_E was calculated in Table 3.2 to be 47.5 weeks. The σ cannot be determined until we know $\Sigma\sigma^2$. This is where we shall start. Specifically, we wish to know the sum of the variances of those activities on the critical path.

In order to determine the variance (σ^2) we use the formula

$$\sigma^2 = \left(\frac{t_p - t_o}{6}\right)^2$$

to determine the variance of each activity. These variances are then totaled to give $\Sigma\sigma^2$.

For ease in calculation, a table can be constructed as shown in Table 3.3.

$$\Sigma\sigma^2 = \Sigma\left(\frac{t_p - t_o}{6}\right)^2 = \frac{563}{(6)^2} = \frac{563}{36} = 15.64$$

Thus 15.64 is the sum of the variances of the critical path activities.

TABLE 3.3

Critical Path Activities					
Successor event	Predecessor event	t_o	t_p	$t_p - t_o$	$(t_p - t_o)^2$
250	240	2	4	2	4
240	200	3	16	13	169
200	150	12	26	14	196
150	130	3	8	5	25
130	110	9	22	13	169
				Total	563

Now we can return to the first formula, which becomes

$$\sigma = \frac{45 - 47.5}{\sigma 15.64}$$

when the known values are inserted. To find the σ of the $\Sigma\sigma^2$ (15.64), we simply take its square root, and thus the equation becomes

$$\sigma = \frac{45 - 47.5}{\sqrt{15.64}}$$

$$\sigma = \frac{-2.5}{3.95}$$

$$\sigma = -.633$$

The figure $-.633$ refers to the number of deviations from the mean (T_E) to the scheduled date (T_S). By referring to Table 3.4, we can convert this σ to the percentage of area under the curve beyond T_S. The figure $-.633$ is between -0.6 and -0.7, and by approximation we can determine that $-.633$ is .26. The figure .26 means that 26 percent of the area under the curve is to the left of T_S (i.e., the shaded area of Figure 3.15). Thus we conclude that there is a 26 percent probability that the project will be completed by the scheduled date.

Generally, probability values of .25 to .30 at the low end of the scale and .60 to .65 at the high end indicate the acceptable range

TABLE 3.4

Table of Normal Distribution

Normal deviate	Area	Normal deviate	Area
−0.0	.50	0.0	.50
−0.1	.46	0.1	.54
−0.2	.42	0.2	.58
−0.3	.38	0.3	.62
−0.4	.34	0.4	.66
−0.5	.31	0.5	.69
−0.6	.27	0.6	.73
−0.7	.24	0.7	.76
−0.8	.21	0.8	.79
−0.9	.18	0.9	.82
−1.0	.16	1.0	.84
−1.1	.14	1.1	.86
−1.2	.12	1.2	.88
−1.3	.10	1.3	.90
−1.4	.08	1.4	.92
−1.5	.07	1.5	.93
−1.6	.05	1.6	.95
−1.7	.04	1.7	.96
−1.8	.04	1.8	.96
−1.9	.03	1.9	.97
−2.0	.02	2.0	.98
−2.1	.02	2.1	.98
−2.2	.01	2.2	.99
−2.3	.01	2.3	.99
−2.4	.01	2.4	.99
−2.5	.01	2.5	.99

of probability. When the calculated probability is below .25 or .30, the likelihood of meeting the project's scheduled completion date is so low that critical path time must be shortened. When probabilities are above .60 or .65, there is a strong likelihood that the project completion date will be met. In cases of very high probability, management should consider using some of the resources committed to the project elsewhere in the company.

3.11   COMPUTER CALCULATIONS

It was noted in the first paragraph of this book that PERT is only one of a number of new management techniques that have been exploited in rapid succession in the decade of the 1950s. Some of the others travel under such euphemistic names as Monte Carlo method, queing theory, linear programming, and simulation.

All of these techniques have in common one predecessor occurrence that makes them practical and without which they would still be mathematicians' playthings. This predecessor is the advent of the electronic computer. All these new techniques require extremely rapid manipulation of massive quantities of data. Brain power did not suddenly increase by some exponential power in the 1950s; what happened was the development of a practical electronic computer, of which such calculations are a forte.

At this point, it is easy to be convinced that a computer would be a real boon to a person who is required to make network calculations. Estimates of the size network that can be readily processed by hand vary from 100 to 150 activities. Larger networks are more efficiently calculated with a computer. Speed in calculation is not the only consideration, however. The many and varied types of computer output reports are of value in themselves. These are discussed in Chapter 4.

The Appendix includes samples of inputs to and outputs from PERT computer programs.

3.12   QUESTIONS

1. Under what set of conditions can slack be negative?

2. Why is it that if slack of a single activity on any path is changed, the slack of the entire path changes by an equal amount?

3.   The formula

$$t_E = \left(\frac{t_o + 4t_m + t_p}{6} \right)$$

gives results that only approximate the results that would be gained by the use of beta analysis, yet it is used by nearly all PERT analysts. Explain.

4.   Why should the largest T_E be used in further calculations when an event has more than one activity arrow leading to it?

5.   Why should the smallest T_L be used in further calculations when an event has more than one successor event?

6.   In a sense, the determination of T_L and T_E are opposite calculations. Explain.

7.   How long would it take to determine the critical path and calculate its slack in a 100-activity network? Could a clerk do this type of work?

3.13   PROBLEMS

1.   Correct at least six errors in the following PERT network.

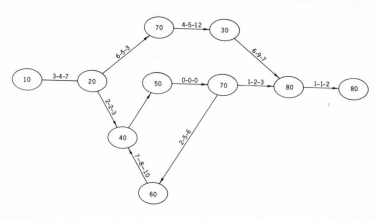

Figure 3.17

2. With the aid of the PERT network below, fill in the blanks of the computation worksheet on page 74 with the appropriate figures.

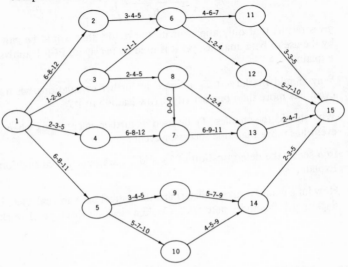

Figure 3.18

3. What is the critical path in Problem 2?

4. Calculate the critical path.

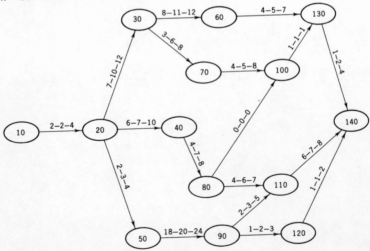

Figure 3.19

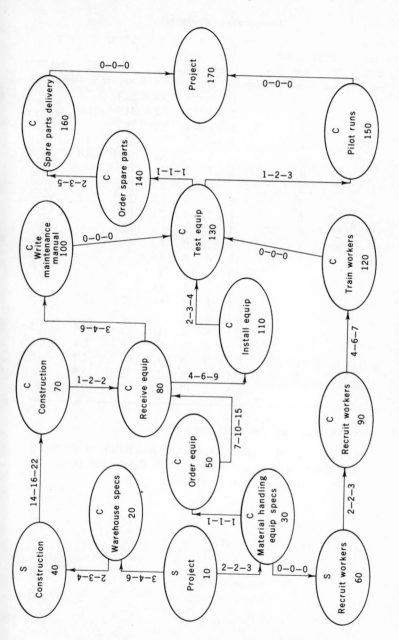

Figure 3.20

73

Computation Worksheet

Successor event	Predecessor event	t_o	t_m	t_p	t_E	T_E	T_L	Slack
15	14	2	3	5	3.2	24.1	24.0	—
	13	2	4	7	4.2	24.5		
	12	5	7	—	7.2	21.7		
	11	3	—	5	3.3	21.4		
14	10	—	5	7	5.5	20.9	20.8	—
	9	5	7	9	7.0	19.2		
13	8	—	—	—	2.2	13.7		
	7	6	9	11	8.8	20.3	19.8	—
12	6	1	2	4	2.2	14.5	—	2.3
11	6	4	6	7	5.8	18.1	—	2.6
10	5	5	7	10	7.2	15.4	—	−0.1
9	5	3	4	5	4.0	—	13.8	1.6
8	7	0	0	0	0.0	—	17.6	6.1
	3	2	4	5	3.8	—		
7	4	6	8	12	—	11.5	11.0	−0.5
6	3	1	1	1	—	3.5		
	—	3	4	5	4.0	12.3	14.6	2.3
5	—	6	8	11	8.2	8.2	8.1	−0.1
	1	2	3	5	3.2	3.2	2.7	−0.5
—	1	1	2	6	2.5	2.5	13.6	11.1
2	1	6	8	12	8.3	8.3	10.6	2.3

5. Calculate the critical path in Figure 3.20.

6. With respect to problem 5, what is the probability of meeting a scheduled time of 40 weeks? What would be the effect on probability if the time were "crashed" to 36 weeks?

4 ▸   NETWORK ANALYSIS

In the foregoing chapters, techniques for determining certain vital facts about a project were introduced. Among the most important findings possible through the PERT network are:

    1.   The amount of time that each activity is likely to consume.

    2.   The earliest time by which each event can be expected to be finished.

    3.   The latest time by which each event can be completed if it is not to cause delay in meeting the scheduled termination date of the project.

    4.   The amount of time, positive or negative, between the time each event is scheduled to be completed and the time allowed by the project termination date.

    5.   The identification of the critical, semicritical, and slack paths throughout the network, and the amount of slack, positive or negative, in each.

    6.   The probability of meeting the scheduled time of the project.

This information is of value only to the extent that it is used. If the process were stopped after gathering figures and calculating, PERT would be interesting, but not dynamic.

The nature of computer reports, how they are used, other means of monitoring the project, and ways in which the time constraint can be met are the subjects of this chapter. In Chapters 2 and 3, hand calculations were mentioned more often than were machine calculations. The choice of which system is used is largely a matter of facilities, technical training of persons involved, and size of network, the computer being almost essential for networks including 150 or more events.

4.1   COMPUTER OUTPUT REPORTS

The PERT analyst garners his information on the progress of the project from the PERT progress printouts of the computer (or through hand calculations in the case of smaller projects or the absence of a computer). Skill in reading and interpreting computer printouts is the forte of the analyst, but other management persons closely connected with the project should develop the ability to read the computer information as usable reports so that little or no translating is necessary. Basic information about the IBM 709 operations is included in the Appendix.

The types of printouts produced by a computer depend upon the program used. The Appendix is fairly typical. It produces four types, each with the same information about the project, but presented in different ways. These are:

1. By successor and predecessor event numbers. Each activity is listed by ascending order of event number. This report is used primarily as a quick way to locate a specific activity when the event numbers bordering it are known.

2. By paths of criticality. Each path is listed in descending order of criticality. The first group of activities listed comprises the critical path. Succeeding listings are other paths listed in descending order of criticality. This output is possible because the computer calculates the various paths through the network and determines the time differences between the end events of paths and the scheduled completion date. In each case, this difference (or slack) determines the degree of criticality of each possible path through the network.

3. By scheduled or latest allowable completion date. Activ-

ities are listed in the order in which they must be completed so that established schedules and the established project completion dates are met. This listing shows the latest allowable date for each activity if it is not to hold up the project. In practice, however, many activities on slack paths should be accomplished earlier than the latest allowable time, since their slack provides a margin of safety.

4.   By department, scheduled or latest allowable date. It was mentioned in Chapter 2 that networks are often coded as to areas of responsibility, either by using different shapes of event bubbles or some other understandable system. This output report is an outgrowth of the input of coded areas of responsibility. Typically, this fourth type of output is divided into coded sections and given to the persons responsible for various portions of the project, so that they can have a continuing record of the extent of their responsibilities and the progress being made.

4.2   REPORTING TO MANAGEMENT

In order to maintain PERT as a dynamic control tool, computer output reports should be distributed to management within hours after the printouts come from the computer. Only in this way can PERT make possible the updated information and improved decision-making for which it has become so well known. In all cases possible, duplication or rewording of reports should be avoided, since this wastes valuable time, adds expense, and dilutes the completeness of original printouts. It is advisable, therefore, that all levels of management involved learn to read and interpret direct computer printouts. A brief explanation at the beginning of the project is usually sufficient training for most managers at least to be able to read printouts.

One area of trouble along this line might be in reports that include data understandable only to the trained statistician. Unexplained variances or standard deviations may fall into this category. Whenever it is necessary that management persons know these figures, some explanation should accompany the reports, but it should be kept brief and be handled in such a way as not to delay report distribution.

Reports to managers should be accompanied by clear indications of what activities or paths need immediate attention to remedy unsatisfactory conditions. If no action is required, that should be stated. All explanations should be brief.

To be effective, project analysis should be a continuing process, starting at the beginning of a project and continuing throughout its life. Ideally, the flow of information, judgments, and actions should form a smooth cycle: from activity changes and revised time

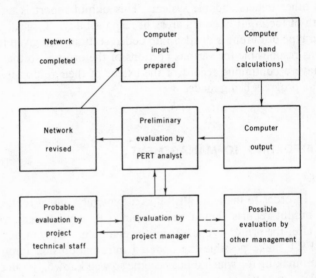

Figure 4.1

estimates, to computer input, to computer (or hand calculations in the absence of a computer), to computer output, to evaluation by the PERT analyst, to evaluation by the project manager, to such other managers as deemed necessary, to the technical staff, and back to activity changes and revised time estimates. Among the persons involved, from PERT analyst to technical staff, there is interplay and frequent exchange of information before the process gets back to the adjustments-and-revised-estimates phase. A rough sketch of the complete cycle is shown in Figure 4.1.

4.3 MONITORING THROUGH DISPLAYS

In addition to computer (or technical hand calculation) reports going to management persons concerned, graphic displays are very useful project monitoring devices. They must be considered auxiliary and secondary to reports, since they are useful in accompanying reports but are seldom used alone. Two types of displays are used more often than others: bar charts and skeleton networks.

Either of these displays is effective for meetings and conferences or for posted progress reports to keep project members informed. Care should be taken, if such presentations are under consideration for management use only, to justify the expense of preparation against the greater value of teaching managers to read computer printouts. Hours of art work and a week or more of delay can be the cost of conveying a point that a practiced eye can ferret from the less glamorous but more detailed direct computer report in a matter of minutes.

Bar charts are made by converting events or groups of events on the critical and semicritical paths into bars. Shaded areas can indicate "to date" progress. Bar charts, as pointed out in the early sections of this book, cannot have pinpoint accuracy or show interdependencies, but for many audiences (employees, boards of trustees, financiers), they are very useful in conveying ideas of general progress.

The skeleton network shows activities on the critical and semicritical paths, and can be drawn to whatever detail deemed necessary, depending upon the audience. Such a network is especially useful to the upper echelons of management who have responsibility for large segments of the project. If the skeleton network can be drawn in fairly accurate proportions, a time scale on a line below it can be helpful in indicating progress. Color coding is sometimes used to identify clearly the critical and semicritical paths, or to suggest transfer of resources from slack to critical paths.

4.4   TIME REDUCTION

Since PERT is a management tool dealing largely with the time constraint, the most important contribution possible through its proper use is time reduction at important points and along longer paths of the network. Six general ways of achieving time reduction are considered in this section:

1. Reduction of the expected time (t_E) of activities on the critical or semicritical paths.
2. Elimination of some parts of the project.
3. Transfer of some resources from slack to more critical paths.
4. Addition of resources.
5. Substitution of one component for another.
6. Parallelization of activities which usually occur in series.

4.41   Reduction of the Expected Time (t_E) of Activities on the Critical and Semicritical Paths.

After these paths have been determined, the time estimates along them can be reviewed. Estimates should not be revised simply because they lie on critical or semicritical paths; this would almost constitute fudging just to make things look better and would be of no permanent value. If the time estimates were sound when first made, they should not be changed upon review unless there is a change in the activity they represent or for some equally good reason.

Some of the reasons for which time estimates might be modified upon review are the addition of extra shifts or men to shorten an activity time, the advent of speedier processing (quicker-drying paint, availability of a more adaptable grade of steel), and better service from outside suppliers (earlier delivery on equipment).

In this connection it should be remembered that time estimates occasionally have to be lengthened because of circumstances unforeseen at the time the estimates were originally made. Who could predict a strike at the plant of an important supplier or a great weather disaster? With good planning, however, opportunities for shortening time estimates should occur much more frequently than should needs for lengthening them.

4.42 Elimination of Some Parts of the Project. This method of reducing time estimates would involve eliminating some nonessential or not-too-essential parts of the project. It was pointed out in Chapter 2 that first networks are drawn to reflect "all normal" conditions. In the interest of speeding the completion of the project, it may be desirable to do a less-than-normal job. In such instances, the risks of change must be compared with the value of the time reduction to ascertain that the exchange should be made.

An example of such an elimination may be the decision not to conduct a series of time-consuming tests in the plant of an equipment manufacturer. Instead, the risk would be taken that the design and fabrication of the equipment were such that flaws would be extremely unlikely, and any that may occur could be corrected during the breaking-in period at the user's plant.

4.43 Transfer of Resources from Slack to More Critical Paths. Application of this method usually involves simply taking resources (people, for example) from activities for which there seems to be excess time and utilizing them in the activities that are causing the tightness in slack on the critical or semicritical paths. After such a move had aided in the reduction of criticality, the resources could be rearranged as originally scheduled.

For example, if a project calls for the design of several new products in order to be able to present a full line, the PERT network may show that the design phase of one product is on the critical path, while those of others are not. In such a situation, it would be prudent to transfer design personnel from work on the products on slack paths in order to speed up the design work on the product which fell on the critical path. Thus the design requirements would be reduced on the critical path without allowing corresponding changes in the design time of other products to hold up the total project.

Raw materials, tools, equipment, and money are among the other resources that can be temporarily or permanently transferred to critical paths to achieve time reduction.

4.44 Addition of Resources. The most common resource added to speed up progress is that of manpower. This is most commonly done through use of overtime for those persons whose skills are needed to shorten the critical path. Other ways of adding human resources are hiring extra employees, using consultants, requesting that suppliers provide manpower for installation of their equipment, and subcontracting work that consumes skills that are in short supply.

Other resources can be added instead of or in addition to manpower, depending on the needs of the situation. Larger laboratory facilities might be rented to hasten the testing of a new product, newly-developed welding tools might hasten the construction of a bridge, or an additional 4000 units of storage space in a computer might hasten the simulation of wear on a new die. The possibilities are many; it is up to management to select that course of action which will bring about the most useful results.

4.45   Substitution of One Component for Another. This may be done either temporarily or permanently. To power a newly designed piece of equipment, it may be desirable to have a motor made up with exactly the characteristics to drive the equipment most efficiently. If the motor installation is on the critical path and is holding up the project, it may be possible to utilize temporarily a motor of approximately the same characteristics as the ideal motor in order to go forward with the project. Later, when the correct motor is available and the time right, the exchange can be made.

Permanent substitution may be in order when, for example, it is discovered that pouring concrete walls is on the critical path and that, by substituting a different brand of concrete, the curing time of the walls can be reduced.

4.46   Parallelization of Activities That Usually Occur in Series. Given a normal amount of time, we would first plan a training program for operators of new equipment and then recruit the trainees. At the cost of a somewhat inefficient training experience, time can be reduced if the two activities are done in parallel; that is, develop the training program while the recruiting is going on and just one step ahead of the actual beginning training experience.

4.5   CONCLUSION

Network analysis resulting in project adjustment and revision is the final objective of all we have discussed in this and the foregoing chapters, to the end that the total project is successfully accomplished.

The first essential in network analysis is the understanding and appreciation of computer printouts or corresponding hand calculations, not only by the PERT analyst and project manager, but by other concerned managers as well. Bar charts and skeleton networks may be used as additional project monitoring devices.

Reduction of time on critical and semicritical paths is the best utilization of PERT, which is basically a time-oriented planning and control device. Among the most effective ways of reducing time requirements are reduction of the expected time of activities, elimination of some parts of the project, transfer of some resources from slack to critical paths, addition of resources, substitution of one component for another, and parallelization of activities which usually occur in series.

4.6   QUESTIONS

1. In what sense is PERT a dynamic tool?

2. Are four types of computer output adequate? What others would you recommend? How would you revise the existing types of output?

3. Are computer reports difficult to read? Would you recommend that management persons other than those vitally concerned learn to read them?

4. Why is it important to get computer reports distributed quickly? Why is speed important for other types of PERT reports?

5. What stage in the cycle of the continuing PERT process is likely to be most time consuming? What stage is likely to be least time consuming?

6. Under what conditions is it permissible to revise a time estimate?

7. Is it a form of retrogression to convert PERT networks and computer reports into bar charts?

8. There is probably some risk associated with the employment of each of the six suggested methods of time reduction. Cite one possible risk for each of the six methods.

5 ▸ PERT AND THE FUTURE

IT HAS BEEN PREDICTED that the present trend of technological change at an accelerated pace in our industrial world will continue into the foreseeable future. The effect of this on industrial operations is a shortened preparation, production, and sales cycle punctuated by frequent changes in process technology and distribution methods.

From management's point of view, this has meant and will continue to mean a greatly increased premium placed upon effective planning and control. This is one of the reasons why PERT has been accepted with such alacrity.

But PERT is merely a component of the present phase of development of management tools. While far superior to the tools it replaced, it too has limitations that will necessitate revisions and improvements in the future.

5.1 WHERE PERT IS AND IS NOT USEFUL

PERT has been described as a planning and control technique that is useful in the administration of those types of projects that are either new or repeated at infrequent intervals. It is especially useful in projects for which the time span is long, or in which objectives or resources change during the life of the project.

PERT *is not useful* for most repetitive production, distribution, or sales activities, except perhaps for setting up the initial operation. PERT would not be used for planning or controlling the assembly of automobiles, their shipment, or the distribution of automobile parts; or in the administration of on-going selling and advertising campaigns of a manufacturing company.

PERT *is useful* in dam construction, shipbuilding, tearing down and rebuilding large pieces of equipment (such as an open hearth or paper-making machine), building, and bridge construction. In the area of marketing, PERT is useful for planning and controlling product design, the launching of new products, and the opening of new outlets.

Even for those situations in which PERT is adjudged a very useful tool, it has its shortcomings and limitations which the user should recognize from the outset.

5.2 MANPOWER, TIME, COST

All projects can be thought of as situations in which management assembles resources (manpower, equipment, materials, financing) and utilizes these resources within limitations of certain constraints (time, cost, quality) in order to gain certain objectives.

The general nature of any project, as described here, is illustrated in Figure 5.1. Three of the several components in this diagram—the manpower resource and the time and cost constraints—tend to concern management most.

The time constraint has been dealt with very adequately through the development of the PERT networking technique. The network graphically displays an entire project in such a way as to keynote time. Calculation of the criticality of the several paths permits an evaluation of the project duration against the time constraint.

This leaves two problem subareas for which planning and control techniques need yet to be devised. These are manpower utilization and cost.

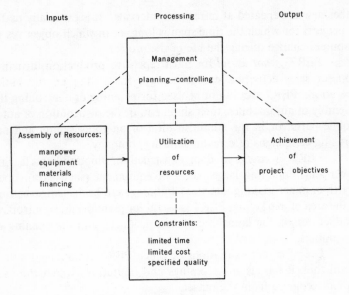

Figure 5.1

5.3   MANPOWER UTILIZATION

Before delving into some of the techniques for manpower utilization, it is useful to have an understanding of the nature of the problem.

A manufacturer desires to build and equip a large modern plant to accommodate the increased sales of his products. His product line consists of a single product with six different models (for example, radios) for which he needs six different assembly lines. Technically, there is no reason why work cannot proceed on the design, acquisition, and installation of the several lines simultaneously. Practically, however, manpower limitations can severely hamper the project.

Assume for simplicity's sake that the manufacturer has available six mechanical engineers. He could assign one engineer to design each line, or he could assign all six to one line, or some combination thereof. Clearly, whatever option he elected would have an effect upon the rest of the project. However, the project need not be very big before spotting the best of various manpower combinations becomes quite difficult. This is so because every small increase in project size is accompanied by a great increase in number of possible manpower combinations.

Fortunately, the electronic computer comes to the manufacturer's aid at this point. He can simulate various assignments of mechanical engineers and other manpower skills on the computer and determine the effect on project objectives.

For the purposes of this discussion, the following assumptions about manpower are made:

1.   Each man has as much creative talent as any other.
2.   Each man is as productive as any other.
3.   The talent and productivity of two or more men is equal to the sum of their individual talents and rates of productivity.
4.   Each man possesses only one skill.
5.   Skills have clear lines of demarcation.
6.   Each activity requires only one manpower skill.

Certainly these assumptions are true only to varying degrees, but they must be made in order to do manpower planning for large projects.

A number of techniques have been developed for facilitating manpower planning and control. At this stage of development, no one technique has general acceptance. One that appears to have promise has been developed by the Space Guidance Center, International Business Machine Corporation, Oswego, New York.[1] The technique permits management to allocate manpower both among and within projects. Within projects management can assign the necessary and available manpower skills and can predict the effect on project objectives if workloads of the assigned personnel are increased. Use of this technique requires predetermination of the minimum and maximum manning limits for each activity, a project completion date, and the total manpower available in each skill category. The schedule calculated is optimum in terms of whole men.

---

[1] A. A. McGee and M. D. Markarian, "Optimum Allocation of Research/Engineering Manpower Within a Multi-Project Organizational Structure," *Institute of Radio Engineers Transactions on Engineering Management*, Vol. EM-9, No. 3, September, 1962, p. 104.

5.4 COST

The fact that PERT does not involve the cost constraint is a major source of dissatisfaction of users who are not involved in defense business, since cost is an even more important factor than time in most nonmilitary work. The problems associated with incorporating cost into PERT are diverse in nature.

One of these problems is caused by the incompatibility of the typical cost system and the activity breakdown of the PERT network. A cost system typically uses a primary breakdown of labor, materials, and overhead with a secondary breakdown of budgets in each of the three primary categories. It is quite unlikely that a cost budget and an activity in the PERT network would cover the same work. Budget accounts are usually much broader than single activities.

Even though this first problem could be overcome (for example, by having one account cover several activities), there are additional difficulties caused by comparing costs against a time scale. As an illustration, even though 60 percent of the cost and time of a project have been consumed, perhaps only 50 percent of the project has been accomplished.

5.5 PERT/COST

By far the most persistent efforts toward overcoming the problems inherent in incorporating cost with PERT have been made by federal agencies. The Department of Defense and the National Aeronautics and Space Administration are the chief contributors. Two guides to PERT/COST systems have been published.[2] These

---

[2] National Aeronautics and Space Administration, *PERT and Companion Cost System Handbook*; and Department of Defense and National Aeronautics and Space Administration, *Guide to PERT/COST Systems Design*; both available from Superintendent of Documents, U.S. Government Printing Office, Washington 25, D.C., at 75 cents each.

systems are used mainly by firms engaged in defense business and are sufficiently complicated to warrant separate study. For this reason, they are not included within the scope of this book, but are readily available for individual examination and study.

5.6   CRITICAL PATH METHOD

The most widely used nonmilitary PERT/COST system is not referred to as PERT by its originators. The Critical Path Method was developed by James E. Kelley and Morgan R. Walker during 1957. It is quite similar to PERT in most respects, the main point of differentiation coming when time estimates are solicited.

The Critical Path Method (CPM) uses two time estimates. When they are solicited, two cost estimates are also requested for each activity. The first time-cost combination sought is for the "all normal" situation for the activity. The time would correspond to the PERT most likely time and the accompanying cost estimate, which is asked for in explicit figures, would be the most probable or most likely cost, both figures covering the same activity in each case. The second time-cost combination requested is the "all crash" situation in which it is assumed that no cost is spared to reduce the time consumed to a minimum for the activity. These two points are shown in Figure 5.2. In the absence of further information in Figure 5.2, a linear relationship is assumed between the two points "all normal" and "all crash." The line parallel to the time axis extending to the right of the "all normal" point is parallel to the time axis because it is assumed that further increases in time would not reduce activity cost. The line parallel to the cost axis extending above the "all crash" point is parallel to the cost axis because it is assumed that further increases in money would not reduce activity time.

After the network is drawn and time and cost information solicited and recorded, the data are processed by computer. The first run is made under "all normal" time and costs. In succeeding schedules produced by the computer, time is compressed so that costs naturally increase. The computer is programmed always to reduce time on the critical path activities which increase cost least

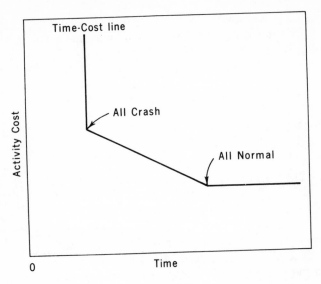

Figure 5.2

when these time reductions are made. Management then selects whichever time-cost schedule best satisfies project requirements.

In addition to the costs which can be directly associated with activities, there are other costs contributing to total project expense, such as overhead, taxes, and selling and administrative expenses. These costs also must be considered before a decision as to which schedule to select can be made. These costs vary only with project life and can be shown as an "indirect cost curve" as in Figure 5.3, on which the "direct cost curve" represents the summation of the individual direct cost lines (one of which is shown in Figure 5.2) for the project.

5.7   CONCLUSION

The breakthrough that led to the PERT planning and control technique in 1958 has been followed by many variations, additions, and revisions. At least 40 were noted by 1962. An evolution of

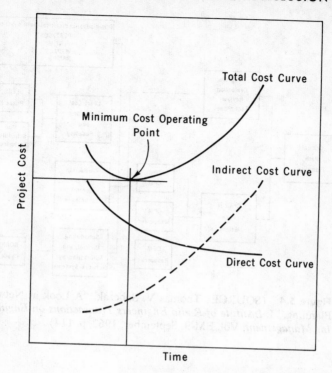

Figure 5.3

critical path techniques, as offered by Thomas V. Sobczak, appears in Figure 5.4. Many of these, like PERT (Program Evaluation and Review Technique), have come to be known by shortened names such as CPM (Critical Path Method), LESS (Least Cost Estimating and Scheduling), PACT (Production Analysis Control Technique), SCANS (Scheduling, Control, and Automation by Network Systems), and RAMPS (Resource Allocation and Manpower Scheduling).

While it is not yet clear which of the manpower and costing techniques will eventually come into general use, or indeed whether organizations will continue to tailor their own special techniques, it is safe to say that the basic PERT technique is here to stay. PERT represents one of the truly significant advances in management techniques during an era when many advances are being made.

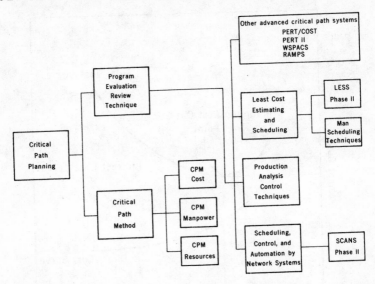

Figure 5.4 (SOURCE: Thomas V. Sobczak, "A Look at Network Planning," I, *Institute of Radio Engineers Transactions on Engineering Management,* Vol. EM-9, September, 1962, p. 114)

5.8 QUESTIONS

1. What general set of conditions has given rise to the development and rapid acceptance by management of the new management science techniques of which PERT is a prime example?

2. What are some specific shortcomings of PERT? Cite specific examples to justify your observations.

3. Explain the probable reasons why the evolutionary development of networking techniques first dealt with the time constraint.

4. Describe the difficulties likely to be encountered in trying to incorporate the cost constraint with PERT.

5. What are some of the reasons why manpower utilization techniques have been slow to develop?

6. Differentiate PERT as a planning and control technique from the production planning and control function that exists in most manufacturing organizations.

7. Cite reasons why you would support or disavow the assumption of linearity between the all crash and all normal points in the CPM technique.

GLOSSARY

Activity   The work required to accomplish an event; depicted on the PERT network by an arrow and identified by the numbers of the events at either end of that arrow (that is, activity 20-30 is represented by an arrow connecting event bubbles 20 and 30).

Arrow   Used to depict an activity.

Bar Chart   A pictorial representation of the work required to complete a project; shows work either in parallel or in series; a predecessor of the PERT network.

Bubble   A circle (or other shape) representing an event on a PERT network.

CPM   A project planning and control technique that deals with both the time and cost constraints.

Critical Path   The longest path through a network.

Dummy Activity   An activity which represents no work or expenditure of time; inserted to maintain the logic of the network.

Event   A specific instant of time, either the start or the completion of a mental or physical task; represented on the PERT network by a bubble, within which is the event number and a brief description, beginning either with *S* (start) or *C* (complete).

94

Gantt Chart   Bar chart named for Henry Gantt, its developer. (*See also* Bar Chart.)

Lead Times   Times assigned to activities in order to give the entire network the desired time relationships; lead times are preceded by the initials *L.T.*

Milestone   An important or key section of a project.

Milestone Chart   An evolutionary step between the bar or Gantt chart in which each long-term job is represented by a bar, and the PERT network in which each small component of a long-term job is represented by a related event bubble; in the milestone chart, bars were broken up into sections (milestones) but were not related to milestones in other bars.

Most Likely Time   The length of time in which an activity could probably be completed.

Network   The PERT project planning device; a pictorial description of the interrelationships of all required events and activities comprising a project.

Optimistic Time   The length of time required for an activity if everything goes perfectly.

Path   A way through the network; identified by the event numbers falling on the path chosen. (*See also* Critical, Semicritical, and Slack.)

Pessimistic Time   The length of time required for an activity if everything possible goes wrong and holds up completion as much as possible.

Predecessor Event   The event immediately preceding the one in question.

PERT   Program Evaluation and Review Technique; a quantitative planning and control device.

PERT/COST   A project planning and control technique that deals with both the time and cost constraints.

Printout   English language output of a computer printer.

Probability   A measure of uncertainty; as used in PERT, an approximation of the likelihood of meeting the scheduled date.

Scheduled Completion Date   The date by which the entire project is scheduled to be finished; the date of the end event if no specific scheduled completion time has been established.

Semicritical Path   A path through the network shorter than the critical path but longer than the slack (shortest) path.

Skeleton Network   A complete but undetailed network showing only the main parts of the total project; used as a basis for drawing detailed networks.

Slack for Any Path   The difference between the latest allowable time and the earliest completion time.

Slack for the Critical Path   The difference in time between the scheduled completion time (or latest allowable time of the end event) of the entire project and the time of the longest path.

Slack Path   The shortest path through the network.

Successor Event   The event immediately following the one in question.

Time Estimate   The approximation of the length of time required to complete an activity.

t_E Expected time.

T_E Earliest expected time.

T_L Latest allowable time.

t_m Most likely time.

t_o Optimistic time.

t_p Pessimistic time.

T_S Scheduled time. (*See also* Scheduled Completion Date.)

SELECTED BIBLIOGRAPHY

Alsaker, E. T., *Network Analysis.* Marietta, Ga.: Lockheed Aircraft Corporation, 1962.

Boulanger, David, "Program Evaluation and Review Technique," *Advanced Management*, July–August, 1961, pp. 8–12.

Clark, C. E., W. Fazar, D. G. Malcolm, and J. H. Rosebaum, "Application of a Technique for Research and Development Program Evaluation," *Journal of Operations Research*, September–October, 1959, pp. 646–669.

Codier, Ernest O., *PERT Application at General Electric Light Military Electronics Department.* Paper presented at A.M.A. Seminar, Saranac, N.Y., September 19, 1961.

Dean, E. L., *Fundamentals of Network Planning and Analysis.* St. Paul: Remington Rand Univac Military Department, July, 1961.

General Electric 225 Application Critical Path Method. Phoenix: General Electric Company Computer Department, 1961.

General Information Manual PERT. White Plains: International Business Machines Corporation Data Processing Division, no date.

Institute of Radio Engineers Transactions on Engineering Management, Vol. EM-9, September, 1962.

The Management Implications of PERT. Chicago: Booz·Allen & Hamilton, Inc., 1962.

Miller, Robert W., "How to Plan and Control with PERT," *Harvard Business Review*, March–April, 1962, pp. 93–104.

Morehouse, W. R., *PERT—An Engineering Program Planning and Analysis Tool,* General Electric Company Technical Information Series No. TIS R59EML63. Utica, N.Y.: General Electric Company, September 15, 1959.

PERT and Companion Cost System Handbook. Washington, D.C.: National Aeronautics and Space Administration, October 30, 1962.

PERT Program Evaluation Research Task Summary Report Phase I. Washington, D.C.: Special Projects Office, Bureau of Naval Weapons, Department of the Navy, September, 1958. Available from Superintendent of Documents, U.S. Government Printing Office; price, $.25.

PERT Programmer's Guide. Sunnyvale, Cal.: Lockheed Aircraft Corporation, September, 1960.

PERT Program Evaluation Research Task Summary Report Phase II. Washington, D.C.: Special Projects Office, Bureau of Naval Weapons, Department of the Navy, September, 1958. Available from Superintendent of Documents, U.S. Government Printing Office; price, $.25.

PERT/COST Systems Design. Washington, D.C.: Office of the Secretary of Defense and National Aeronautics and Space Administration, June, 1962.

APPENDIX

IBM 709 PERT COMPUTER OPERATIONS [1]

THE PERT PROCESSOR PROGRAM performs the various calculations described in Chapter 3 and writes this information on an output tape. The tape is printed to provide the four types of output reports which are described later in this appendix. In order to generate the four types of PERT output reports, the following must be accomplished:

1. Record data.
2. Punch data into detail cards.
3. Punch header cards.
4. Test card input on IBM 1401 preprocessor.
5. Correct card input (if necessary), repeat (4).
6. Process tape output of IBM 1401 on IBM 709.
7. Print tape output of IBM 709 on IBM 1401.

This appendix describes each of these steps.

---

[1] This appendix assumes comprehension of the vocabulary and technique of Chapters 2 and 3. It is intended only as a general guide to computer operations.

1. DATA RECORDING

Exhibit I is the worksheet to be used in preparing input data. The input data, which can be taken from the network in Exhibit II, are:

Column 1   Activity Code. This column contains a code designating the status of the activity. *1* indicates an uncompleted activity, *2* indicates a reestimated activity, and *3* indicates a completed activity.

Columns 2–3   Problem Identification. These columns identify the network to which the data apply. The code may be alphabetical or numerical.

Columns 4–10 and 11–17   Predecessor and Successor Event Numbers. These columns contain the event numbers that bracket the activity for which the data sheet is written. The PERT preprocessor has a limit of six digits each for the predecessor and successor event numbers, so columns 4 and 11 must remain blank in all cases. Activities should be listed by predecessor number, lowest to highest. In cases in which a predecessor has more than one successor, the successors should be listed lowest to highest.

Columns 18–21   Optimistic Time Estimate.

Columns 22–25   Most Likely Time Estimate.

Columns 26–29   Pessimistic Time Estimate.

These columns contain the three time estimates for the activity, expressed in weeks and tenths.

Columns 30–35   Scheduled or Actual Completion Date. If the activity is not complete, but has a scheduled completion date, it is listed in these columns. If the activity has been completed (code *3* in Column 1), the actual completion date must be listed in Columns

Network Title ___TEST PERT NETWORK___   Date __12-24-62__   Prepared by __D. SCANLAN__

2 3 4 * **	PREDECESSOR EVENT	SUCCESSOR EVENT	OPT TIME	MOST LIKELY TIME	PESS. TIME	SCHED/COMP MO DAY YR	ACTIVITY DESCRIPTION	RESPON. CODE
3/1	001	010	00	00	00	0010263	DUMMY, START NETWORK PROGRAM	ENG1
1/1	010	020	50	60	70		DEVELOP BASIC DESIGN	ENG2
1/1	010	030	40	60	70		PREPARE TEST SPECIFICATIONS	ENG1
1/1	020	040	30	60	80		DESIGN MECHANICAL ASSEMBLIES	ENG1
1/1	020	050	70	100	120		DESIGN ELECTRICAL ASSEMBLIES	ENG2
1/1	030	060	60	80	110	0040163	DESIGN TEST EQUIPMENT, SCHED DATE	MFG1
1/1	040	070	80	100	180		FABRICATE MECHANICAL ASSEMBLIES	MFG1
1/1	050	060	10	20	40		LEAD TIME, CPT ELEC EQUIP DESIGN	
1/1	050	080	40	50	70		FABRICATE ELECTRICAL ASSEMBLIES	MFG1
1/1	060	090	80	120	140		FABRICATE TEST EQUIPMENT	MFG2
1/1	070	080	30	40	50		ASSEMBLE MECHANICAL ASSEMBLIES	MFG1
1/1	080	100	10	10	20		FINAL ASSEMBLY	MFG1
1/1	090	100	10	20	40		PREPARE TEST SITE	ENG2
11A12246202								
11B							TEST PERT NETWORK DIAGRAM WITH SCHEDULE DATES, LOCKHEED 709/7090 PROGRAM	

* ACTIVITY CODE   ** CHART DESIGNATION

Exhibit I

101

30–35. If no schedule for actual completion date exists, Columns 30–35 are left blank.

Columns 36–74   Activity Description. These columns describe the activity represented by the predecessor and successor event numbers. In some PERT projects, it may be desirable to record the costs associated with performing the activity. When this is done, the cost figure should be recorded in columns 70–74.

Columns 75–78   Responsibility Code. These columns contain a code to identify the person or department responsible for the activity. The code may be alphabetical, numerical, or a combination of these.

2.   DATA AND HEADER CARDS

Each line (activity) of the Input Data Work Sheet (Exhibit I) generates one IBM card. Thus there will be as many data input cards as there are activities in the network. The first data card is a dummy activity (zero activity time) and always has a 3 in Column 1. The last data card is also a dummy.

Header cards initiate the program and describe the network. Each network deck of data cards requires two header cards.

The *A* header card contains:

Columns	Contents
1	Blank
2–3	Problem identification (letter or number)
4	*A*
5–10	Reference date (month, day, year)

The *B* header card contains:

Columns	Contents
1	Blank
2–3	Problem identification
4	*B*
5–78	Project title

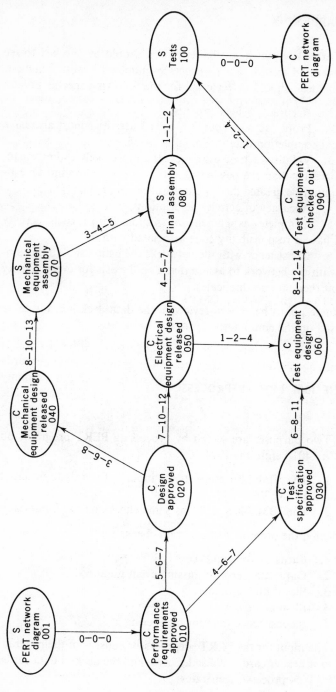

Exhibit II

103

After key punching, the data deck should be checked to see that it is sorted according to preprocessor numbers, lowest to highest. Then the deck should be reviewed for the following specific points:

1. Accuracy of header cards.

2. Proper activity code; all code *3* activities must also have an actual completion date in Columns 30–35.

3. Validity of time estimates; the most likely estimate cannot be greater than the pessimistic estimate and the optimistic estimate cannot be greater than the most likely estimate.

4. Accuracy of activity descriptions.

5. Complete assignment of responsibility; each activity should have a responsibility code associated with it.

6. Consistency with the network; the listing should be compared with the network to assure that a card exists for every activity and that there are no duplicates.

After these points have been reviewed, the data deck is ready to be processed on the computer.

3.   THE IBM 1401 PREPROCESSOR

Two purposes are served by processing PERT programs on the IBM 1401 before the IBM 709:

1. The IBM 1401 converts the input data cards to an input tape for the IBM 709.

2. The IBM 1401 performs some checks on the input data.

Specifically, the preprocessor program checks for:

1. Cards out of sequence.
2. Duplicate, zero, or missing event numbers.
3. Illegal time estimates.
4. Illegitimate dates.
5. Inconsistency in event numbering.

The input for the PERT preprocessor consists of the program deck, an *A* header card, a *B* header card, and the deck of data cards. The PERT preprocessor generates:

1. An input tape for the 709 processor.
2. A check listing of the activities.
3. A preliminary check for a faulty network.
4. A count of activities, events, and errors.

Errors detected by the preprocessor are:

1. Out of sequence; machine halts and prints an *OUT OF SEQUENCE* message beside the activity. The activity must be sorted before the program can be restarted.

2. Missing completion dates; bad time estimates; illegitimate dates; and duplicate, zero, or missing event numbers. Appropriate messages will print beside the activity in question.

3. Inconsistency in event numbering. Every predecessor event must appear as a successor event and vice versa. An appropriate message will print under Phase 2 or Phase 4 on the last page of the output data list.

False errors detected are:

1. Phase 2: will print out the last event number because it lacks a successor event.

2. Phase 4: will print out the first event number because it lacks a predecessor event.

3. Check Date: The program checks all dates against the program date punched in the *B* header card. If any date is equal to it or greater, it will be flagged with *CHECK DATE*.

The PERT preprocessor listing should be reviewed for error messages and appropriate action taken. The format of this listing is shown in Exhibit III. If every event has been linked to a single start and end activity, the predecessor and successor counts should be equal. The error count should equal the sum of the number of *CHECK DATE* messages in the listing, plus any abnormal messages of error printed in the body of the listing or at the end of the listing.

If no errors are found other than the false errors expected, the scratch tape from the PERT preprocessor is then ready to be used as an input tape for the 709 PERT processor program.

T1A1224-6202
T1BTEST PERT NETWORK DIAGRAM WITH SCHEDULE DATES.   CHECK DATE

CHECK DATE

3T1	1	10	0.0	0.0	0.0	01-02-63	DUMMY, START NETWORK DIAGRAM	ENG1
1T1	10	20	5.0	6.0	7.0		DEVELOP BASIC DESIGN	ENG2
1T1	10	30	4.0	6.0	7.0		PREPARE TEST SPECIFICATIONS	ENG1
1T1	20	40	3.0	6.0	8.0		DESIGN MECHANICAL ASSEMBLIES	ENG1
1T1	20	50	7.0	10.0	12.0		DESIGN ELECTRICAL ASSEMBLIES	ENG2

CHECK DATE

1T1	30	60	6.0	8.0	11.0	04-01-63	DESIGN TEST EQUIPMENT, SCHED DATE	MFG1
1T1	40	70	8.0	10.0	18.0		FABRICATE MECHANICAL ASSEMBLIES	
1T1	50	60	1.0	2.0	4.0		LEAD TIME, CPT ELEC EQUIP DESIGN	
1T1	50	80	4.0	5.0	7.0		FABRICATE ELECTRICAL ASSEMBLIES	MFG1
1T1	60	90	8.0	12.0	14.0		FABRICATE TEST EQUIPMENT	MFG2
1T1	70	80	3.0	4.0	5.0		ASSEMBLE MECHANICAL ASSEMBLIES	MFG1
1T1	80	100	1.0	1.0	2.0		FINAL ASSEMBLY	MFG1
1T1	90	100	1.0	2.0	4.0		PREPARE TEST SITE	ENG2

CHECK DATE

1T1	100	999	0.0	0.0	0.0	07-05-63	DUMMY, SCHEDULED DATE TO COMPLETE

END PHASE 1 -- START PHASE 2

END PHASE 2 -- START PHASE 3
END PHASE 3 -- START PHASE 4

3T1000000100000010 00 00 0001026 3DUMMY, START NETWORK DIAGRAM

NO PREDECESSOR FOR EVLNT 0001

END PHASE 4 -- START PHASE 5

ACTIVITY COUNT 14	PREDECESSOR COUNT	SUCCESSOR COUNT 11	ERROR COUNT 2

END PHASE 5

Exhibit III

4.   THE IBM 709 PROCESSOR

The input for the PERT processor is the output tape from the preprocessor and a program tape. Eight tape units are required. The number of activities that can be analyzed is 2048 or fewer. The on-line printer will indicate the start of each of the 14 passes that comprise the program. The on-line printer also indicates the reading of end-of-file marks. At the completion of the job, an *END OF JOB* message will be printed. The B6 tape contains the output. This tape is printed out on the IBM 1401.

5.   COMPUTER OUTPUT REPORTS

The PERT processor program performs various calculations described in Chapter 3 and writes this information on a B6 output tape. This tape is printed to provide output reports for the network.

Four reports are produced. Each provides the same information about each activity, but the activities are arranged in four different ways. The information on each activity, as shown in Exhibit IV, is arranged by columns.

Report 1   By Successor and Predecessor Event Numbers. This report lists each activity in the network in ascending order by event number. It is primarily used as a quick reference listing to locate a specific activity when the predecessor and successor event numbers are known. An example of this listing is shown in Exhibit IV.

Report 2   By Paths of Criticality. The 709 computer calculates the various paths through the network and determines the difference between the expected completion dates. This difference, known as "slack," determines the degree of criticality for each possible path through the network. The second PERT output report lists the activities in ascending order of slack. An example of this report is shown in Exhibit V. The first group of activities in this listing is the critical path. Succeeding paths, listed in order of criticality, are not

PERT SYSTEM

RUN 1
BY SUCCESSOR EVENT NUMBER AND PREDECESSOR EVENT NUMBER.
CHART TI   TEST PERT NETWORK DIAGRAM WITH SCHEDULE DATES.

ENDING EVENT

EVENT PREDECESSOR	SUCCESSOR	NOMENCLATURE	DEP.	DATE EXPECTED	DATE ALLOWED	DATE SCHD/ACT.	PROB.	SLACK	EXP. TIME	EXP. VAR.
0000-001	0000-010	DUMMY, START NETWORK DIAGRAM			11-24-62	A01-02-63		- 5.5	+ 7.3	.1
0000-010	0000-020	DEVELOP BASIC DESIGN	ENG1	02-13-63	01-05-63			- 5.5	+ 7.3	.1
0000-010	0000-030	PREPARE TEST SPECIFICATIONS	ENG2	02-12-63	02-01-63			- 1.5	+ 7.1	.3
0000-020	0000-040	DESIGN MECHANICAL ASSEMBLIES	ENG1	03-26-63	03-14-63			- 1.7	+13.1	.8
0000-020	0000-050	DESIGN ELECTRICAL ASSEMBLIES	ENG1	04-23-63	03-15-63			- 5.5	+17.1	.8
0000-030	0000-060	DESIGN TEST EQUIPMENT, SCHED DATE	ENG2	04-10-63	03-30-63	04-01-63	.09	- 1.5	+15.3	.9
0000-050	0000-060	LEAD TIME, CPT ELEC EQUIP DESIGN		05-08-63	03-30-63			- 5.5	+19.3	1.1
0000-040	0000-070	FABRICATE MECHANICAL ASSEMBLIES	MFG1	06-11-63	05-30-63			- 1.7	+24.1	3-6
0000-050	0000-080	FABRICATE ELECTRICAL ASSEMBLIES	MFG1	05-29-63	06-27-63			+ 4.1	+22.3	1-1
0000-070	0000-080	ASSEMBLE MECHANICAL ASSEMBLIES	MFG1	07-09-63	06-27-63			- 1.7	+28.1	3-7
0000-060	0000-090	FABRICATE TEST EQUIPMENT	MFG2	07-29-63	06-20-63			- 5.5	+31.0	2-1
0000-080	0000-100	FINAL ASSEMBLY	MFG1	07-17-63	07-05-63			- 1.7	+29.3	3-7
0000-090	0000-100	PREPARE TEST SITE	ENG2	08-13-63	07-05-63			- 5.5	+33.1	2-3
0000-100	0000-999	DUMMY, SCHEDULED DATE TO COMPLETE		08-13-63	07-05-63	07-05-63	.01	- 5.5	+33.1	2.3

Exhibit IV

108

RUN 1   ENDING EVENT
BY PATHS OF CRITICALITY
                CHART I1   TEST PERT NETWORK DIAGRAM WITH SCHEDULE DATES.

EVENT PREDECESSOR	SUCCESSOR	NOMENCLATURE	DEP.	DATE EXPECTED	DATE ALLOWED	SCHD/ACT.PROB	SLACK	EXP. TIME	EXP. VAR.
0000-001	0000-010	DUMMY, START NETWORK DIAGRAM		11-24-62	A01-02-63		- 5.5	+	
0000-010	0000-020	DEVELOP BASIC DESIGN	ENG1	02-13-63	01-05-63		- 5.5	+ 7.3	.1
0000-02C	0000-050	DESIGN ELECTRICAL ASSEMBLIES	ENG1	04-23-63	03-15-63		- 5.5	+17.1	.8
0000-050	0000-060	LEAD TIME, CPT ELEC EQUIP DESIGN		05-08-63	03-30-63		- 5.5	+19.3	1.1
0000-060	0000-090	FABRICATE TEST EQUIPMENT	MFG2	07-29-63	06-20-63		- 5.5	+31.0	2.1
0000-090	0000-100	PREPARE TEST SITE	ENG2	08-13-63	07-05-63		- 5.5	+33.1	2.3
0000-100	0000-999	DUMMY, SCHEDULED DATE TO COMPLETE		08-13-63	07-05-63	07-05-63 .01	- 5.5	+33.1	2.3
0000-020	0000-040	DESIGN MECHANICAL ASSEMBLIES	ENG1	03-26-63	03-14-63		- 1.7	+13.1	.8
0000-040	0000-070	FABRICATE MECHANICAL ASSEMBLIES	MFG1	06-11-63	05-30-63		- 1.7	+24.1	3.6
0000-070	0000-080	ASSEMBLE MECHANICAL ASSEMBLIES	MFG1	07-09-63	06-27-63		- 1.7	+28.1	3.7
0000-080	0000-100	FINAL ASSEMBLY	MFG1	07-17-63	07-05-63		- 1.7	+29.3	3.7
0000-010	0000-030	PREPARE TEST SPECIFICATIONS	ENG2	02-12-63	02-01-63		- 1.5	+ 7.1	.3
0000-030	0000-060	DESIGN TEST EQUIPMENT, SCHED DATE	ENG2	04-10-63	03-30-63	04-01-63 .09	- 1.5	+15.3	.9
0000-050	0000-080	FABRICATE ELECTRICAL ASSEMBLIES	MFG1	05-29-63	06-27-63		+ 4.1	+22.3	1.1

Exhibit V

PERT SYSTEM

RUN 1
BY SCHEDULE OR LATEST ALLOWABLE DATE AND SUCCESSOR EVENT NUMBERS.
CHART I1 TEST PERT NETWORK DIAGRAM WITH SCHEDULE DATES.

EVENT PREDECESSOR	SUCCESSOR	NOMENCLATURE	DEP.	EXPECTED	DATE ALLOWED	DATE SCHD/ACT.	PROB	SLACK	EXP. EXP. TIME VAR.
0000-001	0000-010	DUMMY, START NETWORK DIAGRAM							
0000-010	0000-020	DEVELOP BASIC DESIGN	ENG1	02-13-63	11-24-62	A01-02-63		- 5.5 + 7.3	-.1
0000-010	0000-030	PREPARE TEST SPECIFICATIONS	ENG2	02-12-63	01-05-63			- 5.5 + 7.1	.3
0000-020	0000-040	DESIGN MECHANICAL ASSEMBLIES	ENG1	03-26-63	02-01-63			- 1.7 +13.1	.8
0000-020	0000-050	DESIGN ELECTRICAL ASSEMBLIES	ENG1		03-14-63			- 5.5 +17.1	.8
0000-050	0000-060	LEAD TIME, CPI ELEC EQUIP DESIGN	ENG1	04-23-63	03-15-63			- 5.5 +19.3	1.1
0000-030	0000-060	DESIGN TEST EQUIPMENT, SCHED DATE	ENG2	04-10-63	03-30-63	04-01-63	.09	- 1.5 +15.3	.9
0000-040	0000-070	FABRICATE MECHANICAL ASSEMBLIES	MFG1	06-11-63	05-30-63			- 1.7 +24.1	3.6
0000-060	0000-080	FABRICATE TEST EQUIPMENT	MFG2	07-29-63	06-20-63			- 5.5 +31.0	2.1
0000-070	0000-090	ASSEMBLE MECHANICAL ASSEMBLIES	MFG1	07-09-63	06-27-63			- 1.7 +28.1	3.7
0000-060	0000-080	FABRICATE ELECTRICAL ASSEMBLIES	MFG1	05-29-63	07-05-63			+ 4.1 +22.3	1.1
0000-090	0000-050	PREPARE TEST SITE	ENG2	08-13-63	07-05-63			- 5.5 +33.1	2.3
0000-050	0000-100	FINAL ASSEMBLY	MFG1	07-17-63	07-05-63	07-05-63	.01	- 1.7 +29.3	3.7
0000-100	0000-999	DUMMY, SCHEDULED DATE TO COMPLETE		08-13-63	07-05-63			- 5.5 +33.1	2.3

Exhibit VI

110

PERT SYSTEM

RUN 1   ENDING EVENT
BY DEPARTMENT, SCHEDULE OR LATEST ALLOWABLE DATE, AND SUCCESSOR EVENT
CHART T1   TEST PERT NETWORK DIAGRAM WITH SCHEDULE DATES.

EVENT PREDECESSOR	SUCCESSOR	NOMENCLATURE	DEP.	DATE EXPECTED	DATE ALLOWED	DATE SCHD/ACT.	PROB	SLACK	EXP. TIME	EXP. VAR.
0000-010	0000-020	DEVELOP BASIC DESIGN	ENG1	02-13-63	01-05-63			- 5.5	+ 7.3	.1
0000-020	0000-040	DESIGN MECHANICAL ASSEMBLIES	ENG1	03-26-63	03-14-63			- 1.7	+13.1	.8
0000-020	0000-050	DESIGN ELECTRICAL ASSEMBLIES	ENG1	04-23-63	03-15-63			- 5.5	+17.1	.8
0000-010	0000-030	PREPARE TEST SPECIFICATIONS	ENG2	02-12-63	02-01-63			- 1.5	+ 7.1	.3
0000-030	0000-060	DESIGN TEST EQUIPMENT, SCHED DATE	ENG2	04-10-63	03-30-63	04-01-63	.09	- 1.5	+15.3	.9
0000-060	0000-100	PREPARE TEST SITE	ENG2	08-13-63	07-05-63			- 5.5	+33.1	2.3
0000-040	0000-070	FABRICATE MECHANICAL ASSEMBLIES	MFG1	06-11-63	05-30-63			- 1.7	+24.1	3.6
0000-070	0000-080	ASSEMBLE MECHANICAL ASSEMBLIES	MFG1	07-09-63	06-27-63			- 1.7	+28.1	3.7
0000-050	0000-080	FABRICATE ELECTRICAL ASSEMBLIES	MFG1	05-29-63	06-27-63			+ 4.1	+22.3	1.1
0000-080	0000-100	FINAL ASSEMBLY	MFG1	07-17-63	07-05-63			- 1.7	+29.3	3.7
0000-060	0000-090	FABRICATE TEST EQUIPMENT	MFG2	07-29-63	06-20-63			- 5.5	+31.0	2.1
0000-001	0000-010	DUMMY, START NETWORK DIAGRAM			11-24-62	A01-02-63		- 5.5	+	
0000-050	0000-060	LEAD TIME, CPI ELEC EQUIP DESIGN		05-08-63	03-30-63			- 5.5	+19.3	1.1
0000-100	0000-999	DUMMY, SCHEDULED DATE TO COMPLETE		08-13-63	07-05-63	07-05-63	.01	- 5.5	+33.1	2.3

Exhibit VII

111

shown as complete paths, but rather as variations of the first critical path.

Report 3   By Schedule or Latest Allowable Completion Date. This report, shown in Exhibit VI, lists the activities in the order that they must be completed by in order to meet established schedule dates, and meet the established project completion date. The listing is the latest allowable schedule for the job if all intermediate schedule dates have been revised to be equal to or earlier than the latest allowable date. In actual practice, however, many activities with positive slack should be completed before the latest allowable date to avoid an excessive demand on available resources and to provide a margin of safety.

Report 4   By Department, Scheduled or Latest Allowable Date. This report, shown in Exhibit VII, lists the activities according to the responsibility code used in the network. This report is typically broken down into sections and given to the persons responsible for various portions of the project so that they have a record of the scope of their responsibilities in the project and the schedule requirements for completion of their assigned tasks.